Malcolm and Me

Malcolm and Me

LIFE IN THE LITTER BOX

William J. Thomas

McArthur & Company

Toronto

This paperback edition published in 2004 by
McArthur & Company
322 King Street West, Suite 402
Toronto, Ontario
M5V 1J2
www.mcarthur-co.com

Library and Archives Canada Cataloguing in Publication

Thomas, William J., 1946-
  Malcolm and me : life in the litter box / William J. Thomas.

First published: Toronto : Stoddart, 1993.
ISBN 1-55278-470-3

    1. Malcolm (Cat) 2. Cats—Humour. 3. Canadian wit and humour
(English) I. Title.

PS8589.H471Z47 2004   C818'.5402   C2004-904240-8

Design and Composition: Michael P.M. Callaghan
Cover Photo: William J. Thomas
Printed in Canada by: Friesens

The publisher would like to acknowledge the financial support of the
Government of Canada through the Book Publishing Industry Development
Program, The Canada Council for the Arts, and the Ontario Arts Council for
our publishing activities. We also acknowledge the Government of Ontario
through the Ontario Media Development Corporation Ontario Book Initiative.

10 9 8 7 6 5 4 3 2 1

This book is dedicated to two Malcolms and a Nancy,
who add up to one cat, a wife and three friends

CONTENTS

ACKNOWLEDGEMENTS

I hate acknowledgement pages. I flip by the acknowledgements page of any book as quickly as I change the channel of every television awards program as soon as somebody says "I would like to thank . . ." So unless you think there's the tiniest, slightest, remotest possibility that your name is going to be mentioned on this page—blow right on by.

Now that I've got rid of all those fair-weather friends, I would like to thank the Malcolm Wranglers—people who fed, watered, babysat and passed my ultimatums along to him while I was often not at home—Murray the Cop, Tom Pierce, John Tryfiak, Diane Bisson and Pat Gagno.

A big thanks to Debbie Kallender of the Welland Library who gives me so much time and assistance that she should be fired immediately.

I would like to acknowledge my most faithful reader, Eleanor Hyatt, who clips all my columns and sends them to her relatives in Nova Scotia, who now owe me several thousand dollars in lost print revenues. Thank you Karen Rempel Arthur who dropped her own writing to transfer this book to disk.

To Monica Rose, who didn't have to like cats to love Malcolm—thank you.

Thanks to David Barlow, not that he ever did anything for Malcolm. I just like the guy.

To Dr. David Thorne, Malcolm's vet and the Marcus Welby of the pet world—thank you for such care and special attention.

To Don Bastian, who dared to travel where other editors preferred to pass—thank you.

No thanks to Barry Thomas, who, after I had Malcolm neutered, constantly embarrassed him by calling him No-Nuts.

To my agent Daphne Hart, who saw new life in works gone by — thank you for singing my praises for publishers everywhere. Hey, some of it's actually true.

And to my new best friend and publisher Kim McArthur—thank you for treating my books the way I'd hoped they'd be handled the first time around. Out of nowhere came Kim with a contract in hand and gave me a very kind kick in the ass, which I badly needed—thank you. Kim laughs out loud whenever I walk into her loft and I pray it's my writing and not the pants I'm wearing.

1
MALCOLM AND ME

I never cared for cats.

I loved dogs—big dogs like Bobby, our neighbour's smart and gentle collie in the village of Dain City, where I grew up. No kid from Dain City ever learned to skate on the pond behind our house without a week of hanging on to Bobby.

I loved medium-sized dogs like Penny, for sixteen years our reddish-blond family mutt, with his teeth pushed in by a motorcycle and a body that wiggled, danced, jumped and rolled over at the sight of anybody's outstretched hand.

I loved tiny dogs like Paddy, Penny's chihuahua's step-brother who, on a hot summer's day, would chase circular streams of water from the lawn sprinkler until he passed out. He was killed by a car with those blue "sex" lights that had to swerve across one full lane and several feet into our driveway to hit him. I'm still looking for that car with those blue "sex" lights.

I loved dogs.

But I never much cared for cats. Not until I married a woman who loved cats. I wanted a dog. She wanted a cat. So we compromised—we got two cats. When the marriage ended she got one cat and a '67 Cutlass Convertible. I wound up with Malcolm.

Malcolm was definitely not my idea.

I once had a real cat—a big, tough, fluffy tabby by the name of Floyd, who came when he was called, yammered back at you when you spoke to him, tortured frogs in his spare time. Early on, however, it was pointed out to me by my wife that Floyd needed a buddy. The fear here was that without strong male companionship Floyd could turn out to be a mama's kitten and later, of course, a latch-key cat. The intimated concern was for his manhood—something that later was taken care of with two swift swipes of a veterinarian's scalpel at precisely $17.50 per swipe.

Nonetheless, a fay feline I did not need, so I quietly acquiesced.

At that time my wife was a teacher, and every day on her way to work she would see this cute handful of a kitten sitting at the end of a driveway near the main road that went from Fonthill to Welland, Ontario. The mother and the rest of her litter she spotted up near the house, but this one particular curious little waif just sat on the sidewalk watching the world go by. (I now know he was memorizing the makes and models of food trucks that he might hijack when he got bigger.)

When the time was right we made the offer, and this little loner was ours. (Years later this transaction would become living proof of the "Be careful what you wish for" principle.)

Malcolm was a medium-grey short-haired, with deep, dark tiger-stripe markings around his face and feet. He was full of himself and anything that could remotely be described as food. When he wasn't eating, Malcolm would sit and stare at furniture and household appliances wondering how long it would take for them to deteriorate to the point of edibility. Sometimes, after I'd been motionless for a couple of hours, say, reading a book, I'd look up to see Malcolm looking at me with hunger in his eyes, and I would get very nervous.

He had big, beautiful, emerald eyes—all shyness and innocence, even when he was bad. Especially when he was bad.

Malcolm was long and thin when he stretched out, but he looked full and fat when he hunched himself on all fours.

We were told by people in the house where he was born that not long after he learned to walk he got caught in a screen door, sending forth a scream that hit a high F and shattered milk bowls all over the neighbourhood. Thereafter, although he was in no pain, his rear-end assembly seemed to have an itinerary not necessary approved by the front part of his body. There *was* communication between his front and back legs, but the signals seemed to come through a third party with a mischievous sense of humour. He walked just like John Wayne, and for years I'd try to coax him into saying, "Well, circle the wagons, Pilgrim, or we're dead where we sit!" But he wouldn't. Malcolm has a real stubborn streak in him.

When Malcolm ran, his right front leg and right back leg shot forward simultaneously, to be followed by his left front leg and left back leg, just like a standardbred pacer.

Essentially that was Malcolm, not talented enough to nail down a speaking part in a western, not big enough to pull a sulky around a half-mile oval track.

I liked Malcolm. To me he wasn't so much a cat as a cartoon character that had been kicked out of a comic strip for stealing the artist's lunch.

So, enter Malcolm, Floyd's designated buddy, walking like a Slinky toy and smiling like a buck-toothed Cheshire at the sight of two square meals a day and a litter-lined pot to pee in. We had high hopes for this male-bonding match-up when I brought Malcolm home. Floyd spat at him immediately and never went near him again. In hindsight, I'd have to admit that Floyd was an immensely better judge of character than I.

Malcolm wasn't good at sharing and he never really grasped the concept of the "two-bowl, two-cat" system. He liked to think of it more as an "all-you-can-eat buffet." Losing sleep and eating only whatever Malcolm spilled, Floyd went into decline. His happiness decreased in inverse proportion to Malcolm's weight.

Time passed. Though the marriage didn't make it, strangely enough Malcolm did—all the way into my new rural route mailbox on Sunset Bay in Wainfleet, Ontario. He just showed up one day dragging twenty pounds of cat litter and four ounces of homegrown catnip he had hidden in the bag. Eyewitnesses reported seeing a woman leaving the drop-and-run scene who looked suspiciously like my former wife, driving a two-door convertible that was suspiciously no longer mine.

There was no mistaking Malcolm, however, swaggering like The Duke and smiling with an overbite that would cause a vampire to cry out with envy.

That was 1980, and Malcolm was six years old, or forty-two in human years. I was thirty-three in human years, almost five in cat years. So, given some cross-wired chromosomes and our common aversion to arithmetic, we were roughly the same age. The big difference was that my mother cared enough to call once in a while to see how I was doing.

Since then we've been through veritable hell together, Malcolm and me: the Blizzard of '77; the Great Flood of '85; two knee operations (mine, not his); a traumatic castration (his, not mine). He's been dewormed, deflea'd—and considerably depressed since a possum under the house partially succeeded in ripping out his tongue one winter, something I'd been threatening to do ever since I met him.

The possum, a mother with babies to protect, had bitten clear through Malcolm's tongue in a prolonged eviction fight. When I finally wrestled him out from under the house, I cleaned up all the cuts and blood—but I never thought to look in his mouth. In the three days it took for gangrene to blacken a good portion of his tongue, he still managed to eat every meal. Otherwise, I'd have been ever so suspicious.

Dr. David Thorne went white when I carried Malcolm into the clinic with this piece of black meat sticking out the side of his mouth. The good doctor rushed him into surgery immediately, cautioning me to expect the worst: he'd never seen anything quite like this, he said. Yet thanks to the miracle of modern veterinary medicine (and a cheque for $214), Malcolm survived the operation. And he still had half a tongue.

When he arrived home from the clinic two days later, he was visibly weak. He staggered, he weaved, he stumbled, he mumbled, but when he finally collapsed he managed to get most of his face clearly over the rim of his food bowl for a touchdown. Yes, his record remained intact: except under an anaesthetic, Malcolm has never missed a meal in his life.

As I said, I like Malcolm, but *like* is a rather weak endorsement for living together. Carrying my last name and sleeping in my bed is more an arrangement of convenience (his, not mine) than a true love affair.

In fact, Malcolm is an unending source of embarrassment to me. At the Clarence Street Veterinary Clinic in nearby Port Colborne, the receptionist announces him as "Malcolm Thomas," an insult made worse by the awful fact that he's the closest thing I have to a real son. (Plus, as I've already explained, he's about nine human years older than me.)

Whenever I have friends to the house, Malcolm routinely drops a dead rodent at their feet, acting every bit the fearless predator—though he's way too slow to catch one: these little corpses all have tiny tread marks on them where they've been hit by several cars.

Then there's the late-night horror scene in which he bolts upright in bed and lets loose a blood-curdling scream to ward off a stray who has encroached his territory and been spotted through the sliding glass door. The first time this happened I thought he was dying; the second time only a cluttered crawl-space kept me from killing him.

It's safe to say that Malcolm is the only cat in captivity who has spent most of his adult life in the doghouse.

But in every failing relationship each must accept some of the blame. I too am guilty. For one entire year a cat food company ran a promotion in which I would send them ten labels and they would rebate me one dollar. Instead of duti-fully depositing the refunds in Malcolm's food jar, I was stash-ing the cash and stopping at the Belmont Hotel for a couple of beers after work.

Small-town living being what it is, Malcolm somehow found out. He promptly peed on my tennis shoes. Then he began consistently overshooting the end of his litter box, and he invented a game called Hide the Hairball. In this and every other war I got into with Malcolm, well, you could just call

me Saddam. (Don't be fooled by the soft fur and the big eyes —a cat carrying a grudge harbours a virtual arsenal of weaponry in that little body.)

I tried to enact a truce by showering him with cat toys, but he just drooled on them until they all rusted and stuck together. I promised him tickets to a professional cat show. I promised him his own canary. I even brought home a bouquet of freshly cut catnip. But nothing worked until those dollar bills started filling up his food jar.

Malcolm may have been an accountant in another life; he has that blood-from-stone stubbornness about him.

Yet we continue to live together under the same roof. Malcolm scarfs down one tin of cat food every day and buries his face in a quart of milk every week, but to him I'm just the guy who operates the can opener.

Still, I can't get home early enough, I can't fill his food bowl fast enough. Sometimes I look at Malcolm and think: If I really wanted to be abused, used and hassled every time I walked in the door—hey! I could have stayed married.

Yet without any options and with only each other, we set up house together. Looking back, it was a touching story, really, a story of what I consider to be a single, highly intelligent male and master of the universe creating an ingenious system of cohabitation and laying down the rules and regulations for peaceful coexistence.

After all the years I must admit I broke a few of his rules, but he could never really prove anything. I must admit that when it came to sensitivity and companionship Malcolm knew when I was down. Malcolm knew when I was feeling blue and needed a little hug. He didn't give a shit, of course. But he knew.

2

BRINGING UP
MALCOLM

Roaming through my neighbourhood lately is a cast of classless cats. They come for my Malcolm.

One cat wants desperately to make love to Malcolm, two young Turks want to beat him to a pulp, and I suspect K.C.—the seal point Siamese who is so dumb the breeders' association has taken the unusual step of revoking his papers—could go either way on this one. If he had a mind to, which he most definitely does not.

The rust-coloured, sweet-faced female, who preens herself just outside every door and window in the house between three and six every morning, does not realize that Malcolm's reproductive equipment was surgically altered many years ago, leaving him unhappy and unhorny but non-spraying and home-loving. He's a eunuch, really.

The two young grey-striped usurpers to the community's cat crown have no respect for Malcolm's war record, they pay no homage to his awkward walk, have no regard for gnarled gums that once held teeth. They do not understand that every notch in Malcolm's ears is a medal won in combat.

They are upstart gunslingers looking to make a name. Malcolm's the sheriff who'd rather retire but the town won't let him, because this is his town, his territory, and instinctively he'll fight to protect it. He must. He's a cat. (Which is a lot more than can be said for K.C., the Siamese who thinks he's a dog with non-life-threatening behavioural disorders!)

But Malcolm's got class.

He never goes near the road. He tried at first, but repeated attacks by a hooded terrorist (that would be me) setting off cherry bombs in the ditch between him and the pavement have convinced Malcolm that that thoroughfare is not just a country road, it's a road with landmines in a country that's at war.

He never strays beyond his designated territory of my house and the three summer cottages on each side of me. He used to, but after several ambushes by a wacko in a cowboy hat with a starter's pistol (that would be me again) Malcolm is certain that the city limits of Detroit start 100 yards to the west, Miami just behind him to the east. I know. Sometimes in the summer while walking barefoot with a tray full of beer, I've stepped on one of his survey markers.

Malcolm does not venture near the shores of the lake, even though he watched with great curiosity—as we all did—last winter while Duh the Siamese was pulled off a mound of ice just as he was about to pounce on a seagull drifting in five feet of water below.

Territorial limits excepted, Malcolm does his business only in the properly designated and regularly inspected litter box. It wasn't always that way. Once, as a way of punishing me for taking a transatlantic trip (he had no way of knowing Air Canada was already taking care of that), he started doing number one in the bathtub. The house-sitter described how he'd dash down the hall, hit the linoleum floor, leap into the tub, take a quick tinkle and be out of there in less than half a minute. (Old people envy this story.)

But then some sicko with a rubber plug and a criminal mind (that would be me once more) filled the tub with water on his next trip out of town. The house-sitter described the mad dash, the linoleum slide, the grand leap . . . and then . . . and then she heard what sounded like a fat man drowning in a vat of beer. Malcolm came out coughing, sputtering, drenched to the ears and shaking himself off for hours.

But Malcolm came out a better-behaved cat. Now he knows the litter box is for peeing and the bathtub is probably where Jimmy Hoffa got it. Now it's like a Pavlovian experiment. I run water in the tub and he runs for the box in the back hall. Rodney Dangerfield once defined class as a guy who gets out of the shower to take a wizz. Malcolm has class.

When Malcolm was a kitten and I was a married man, he started begging for food at the table. No luck there, he began jumping up on the kitchen counter. He stopped that habit in a helluva hurry. He found out the hard way, just like I did— that's where my wife's cooking was.

Later, he took to rummaging through the kitchen garbage late at night for things like chicken bones and clam shells, until some sadist (you guessed it) rigged an oversized mechanical mouse in the garbage pail, the kind that shrieks bloody murder and gets up to 60 m.p.h. in twelve seconds on any surface, including linoleum. I didn't see it happen, I just heard the Monster Mouse kick in, and the next thing I saw was Malcolm burrowing under the bedsheets.

Now Malcolm knows that his food is in his dish and that the garbage pail is where they filmed *Alien II*.

Later still, his jumping up on furniture necessitated the "collapsing chair" routine, and his jumping up on the stereo gave rise to the "hair-trigger fire truck siren."

And each time, Malcolm emerged a better cat. A cat with discipline and depth. All right, so he's got a twitch on the right side of his face and he spends his day shivering in a corner fearing the next land mine, the next trip switch . . . Still and all, he is very well behaved.

He may be neurotic but he's not a nuisance, which is more than I can say for those other rubes who keep trespassing on his territory. It just goes to show you what a little discipline can do to train a pet. That and a good gag store.

Yet life as Malcolm knew it did a backward somersault the day "the kid" walked into town. This brash little seal point Siamese, a few months old at the time, walked up to the screen door of my kitchen and started growling and gurgling and walking in circles and generally threatening Malcolm with all manner of murderous things, including death by strangulation with a flea collar.

Malcolm observed this "Dance of the Stupid Seal Point" with an amused grin until he finished his breakfast of warmed-over Texas Ranch Grill. Upon exiting onto the patio, Malcolm lumbered up to the Siamese and landed one haymaker of a right-paw that sent the rookie through a row of roses and up against the cement cap of an old water well. It was the kind of thing you'd expect John Wayne to do to Ricky Nelson in *Rio Bravo*.

Shortly, when his vision returned and the ringing in his ears eased up, K.C. picked himself up and went home, absolutely disgusted that his grand gesture to meet the neighbour should be rebuffed with a roundhouse right and a threatening hiss, indicating there was more where that came from.

He didn't come back. Not until the next morning, when the whole damned thing happened all over again. Except this time Malcolm had been eating Seafood Surprise for breakfast, and when K.C. ducked a hard right, Malcolm caught him with a solid left that put him in a small rock garden scratching madly for traction on a railroad tie to distance himself from this . . . this *brute* who was highly antagonistic and, by all accounts, ambidextrous.

So, for well over a year, it has gone on like that. K.C.—the cat who thinks he's a displaced chihuahua with a meow— loves, worships and idolizes Malcolm. He wants desperately to play with him. Malcolm would just as soon sit on a cactus plant as look at this little jerk. Malcolm loves K.C. the way a new bronze statue loves a pigeon, the way toads love curbs, the way Canada still loves Brian Mulroney.

But the kid's not a quitter. Either this Siamese is the most determined seal point born to the breed or he's even dumber than most people give him credit for. (And believe me, they are unanimous and lavish in their praise of his absence of smarts.) And you know, I think the kid is winning. I do. In a prolonged war of wills that spans the territory of seven cottages, complete with sand beach, a creekbed and abandoned outhouses, it's the little things you notice.

Oh, Malcolm still knocks him around once in a while, but it's more out of boredom than vengeance and there's no sting in his punches. There's no hissing anymore, the tail doesn't swell up, and fur fails to rise on his back. It's just an occasional half-hearted reminder—*bang!*—sharp clip behind the ear!—that says: "We are not buddies, I don't much like you, and play is something between a witless kitten and a ball of string."

"Quick, look over there, K.C.!" *Whack!* "Grow up, dummy!"

But the kid won't quit. Malcolm makes his morning rounds under cottages, inspecting storage sheds and tramping through clumps of bushes where field mice live at no risk whatsoever and he returns covered in cobwebs, with dead flies in his ears. Three strides behind him comes K.C., covered in cobwebs, with dead flies in his ears.

Sometimes they just lie a few feet apart on the sun-hot patio bricks, Malcolm sleeping and K.C. sleeping with one eye open, ever expectant of that unprovoked rap on the head. Suspicious of each other but sleeping together, they're very much like a coalition government.

But last June, the visits suddenly ended.

K.C. was hit by a car. Malcolm seemed confused but pleased with his renewed peace and quiet. Then K.C. made a miraculous recovery. Out of clinic and out of traction, his first stop was my kitchen door. K.C. had that longing look of reunion on his face, the kind of expression you see in a newspaper photo taken at an airport of seventy-five-year-old Romanian brothers separated at birth.

Malcolm caught him with a short, quick jab to the noggin. *Bang!* "Welcome home, cheese brain."

The lady from Burlington who ran over K.C. did the hard and decent thing: she stopped and reported the incident. I have her name. I'm not paranoid by any means, but at this time I am checking to see if her home phone number shows up on any of my telephone bills prior to the accident.

It's just a hunch and I'm not accusing anybody, but given the relationship between Malcolm and the kid, I'm looking into the possibility that it may have been a contract hit.

Malcolm seemed awful nervous when K.C. showed up at the door again today.

3

I'M NOT A MORNING PERSON BUT MY CAT IS

According to trend forecasters (who are actually weather forecasters who got bored making a lot of money by coming on television every evening at suppertime and predicting "fifty percent chance of precipitation"), we the people of the Western industrialized world are undergoing a profound metamorphosis.

As a social group we are *cocooning* and *burrowing* and *tunnelling* like never before in our development. In other words, with space-age technology at our fingertips and with instant access to all the knowledge the world has amassed since the beginning of time, we've begun to behave like insects trapped in a fourth grader's science fair project. Is this a good idea?

I have no idea what *cocooning* means, but if we start to sleep in ceiling corners of the house, trap each other in giant cobwebs and bite each other on the bum—I, for one, will be calling for the imprisonment of cartoonist Gary Larson. He ought to keep his weird ideas to himself so as not to excite the trend forecasters.

On the matter of living together, statistics show that today more singles are settling into common-law living arrangements and more divorced people are getting married again. And just where does that leave me? I live with a buck-toothed cat who thinks the sound of the electric can opener is the source of all life and the universe itself. Is this a healthy relationship?

It's certainly a phenomenon that even U.S. fad forecaster Faith Popcorn (and yes, that's her real name) dares not broach.

Malcolm drools like a faucet with a worn-out washer. He occasionally trips over the front step and bangs his head on the door. He's lost most of his lower teeth from coming down trees frontward. He's a prime candidate for regular and repeated rinsings with mouthwash. On top of that, he has fleas and snores.

And the worst is, I love him to death.

This variance of reason disturbs me. I'm tempted to write a deeply psychological and trendy little book entitled *Pets Who Disgust People and the People Who Love Them*. Unfortunately, this book would appeal only to the very cerebral, and therein lies the problem—so few cats take the time to read books anymore.

As do all who cohabit, Malcolm and I have fallen into some daily routines that have so far served us both quite well.

At precisely 7 a.m. Malcolm gives me a soft shot in the head and bolts out of bed. Quickly I grab for a book or the alarm clock to try to nail the little bugger before he can escape the bedroom, but I'm always a little late. I then beg, threaten and make wild promises of trips to the Toronto Zoo if he'll come back to bed because I'm too tired to get up and feed him.

Malcolm is not, as they say, light on his feet. When he begins running laps around the house it sounds like two dwarfs doing wind sprints in my living room. It's a scary thought, but in the grey drowsiness of dawn an ordinary house cat can actually convince a person that there are oxen loose in another part of the house.

Mission accomplished: his day is off to a flying start while I stumble down the hall to the john mumbling insults and mentioning by name his mother and father. Malcolm's laps act as a laxative, and by the old clock radio on the headboard I know I have until 7:04 to get him fed and out the door before he wreaks havoc on the litter box.

The feline litter box is little more than an aboveground open-air waste dump. If you've ever looked into the eyes of

a cat using a litter box (something I urge everyone to do once), you will know the meaning of domesticated humiliation. The hurt of a million years of forcing a species of wild animals to live indoors, wear bells around their necks and pretend to enjoy chasing plastic wind-up toys burns from the eyes of a cat hunched in a litter box. Although I have never been fond of the litter box, Malcolm is clearly embarrassed by it.

Toilet training has always been a real problem for Malcolm. As a kitten, he adapted quickly to paper training, but it took me several months to convince him that wallpaper did not count.

I also hate to clean out the litter box. I'd much rather he do his business where he is supposed to do it—in the neighbour's flower garden. Ever since I trained Malcolm to go there, four-foot peonies have sprung up in that garden. And the owners attribute it to the rich black loam of Wainfleet! They're not entirely wrong, but believe me, that loam is a lot blacker and richer since Malcolm came to town.

The rap on the head, the crying, the romping noise—all this is forgiven by the time I open the pantry door and scan a myriad of tasty titles on tin cans, like Savory Stew, Pâté Deluxe, Ranch Supper, Beef Wellington and Chicken á la King.

Malcolm stops running long enough to sit on the floor looking up at the shelf of cat food cans as though he is in some way part of the decision-making process. Yet in all the thousands of times we've done this he has never once said anything, winked, nodded or shaken his head in disagreement.

Yet he looks like he knows exactly what's going on here. Therefore, I can only assume that I have guessed correctly 5,130-odd days in a row. With this kind of streak on the line, I'm starting to feel the pressure. I live in dread that any day now as I come away from the cupboard with the can, I'm going to hear: "You jerk! Don't you know how rich that Fancy Feast is first thing in the morning!" But so far, so good. I'm on a roll.

At 7:03 I have one hand on the lever of the can opener, the other on a rotating can of Mixed Grill Surprise, and I am acutely aware of one thing: the people working for cat food companies who think up names like Seafood Surprise and Beef Ragout are not the same people on the processing line who have to stand close enough to smell that stuff. You can wake up and smell the coffee, but one whiff of Texas Ranch Buffet and you may never sleep again.

There follows a well-choreographed dance scene with "THE GUY WHO CAN WORK THE CAN OPENER" and starring "THE CAT WHO COULD EAT CLEVELAND."

At 7:04 the kettle starts to whistle. Coffee? I should be so lucky. Malcolm has sensitive gums, an absence of strategic teeth and only half a tongue. That's right, the water's for the gravy. I warm up his breakfast for him. Is this pushing the envelope of the eccentric and certifiably whacked or what? Even Roy Rogers, who loved Trigger so much he had the damn horse stuffed when he died, didn't warm up his bag of oats for him!

It's 7:05 and I am stirring warm water into a bowl of revolting mush while Malcolm bumps and grinds circles and reaches up to the countertop, all the while screaming bloody murder. You have to understand that Malcolm eats from the Canadian Veterinarians' list of eight basic food groups recommended daily diet for felines, and more than once, out of sheer impatience, he's actually eaten the list.

The critical moment of the morning is 7:05. The familiar noises of the can opener and the kettle excite Malcolm to a frenzy. He's circling the kitchen in ever-shrinking circles and now screaming loud enough to initiate an animal rights investigation. At this point he could go either way.

My hands are pouring and stirring with the dexterity of a short-order cook in a crowded diner and my feet are moving faster than an Argentine soccer star's. At all costs I must keep Malcolm from getting into the back hall where the litter box sits, so far unscathed. As delirious as he is over the prospect of food, Malcolm's got to go real bad by now and his loyalties lie halfway between the box and the bowl.

I have gone, in less than five minutes, from a relaxed peaceful position to a heart rate of 140. Some guys jog in the morning; I feed my cat.

Risking loss of fingers, I lunge for his dining mat and place the bowl down quickly, jumping back to avoid being splashed as Malcolm does a near-perfect jackknife dive into the dish. I move to higher ground on the patio and watch the whole thing through the safety of sliding glass doors.

It's all over in thirty seconds. The noise emitted in this mass inhalation of warm slop is somewhere between the rutting of two elderly elk and the sound of a French Legionnaire dying slowly in the Sahara. Malcolm doesn't eat his food as much as he snorts, chortles, scarfs, gargles and ingests it upright. On a good day some of the food may find its way into his mouth.

At 7:06 he's out the door, and the litter box has been spared yet again. God, I love it when a plan comes together.

If it wasn't so early I'd crack the champagne, but I celebrate instead by pouring the rest of the lukewarm water onto brown coffee crystals and stir them until steamy and grey.

At 7:07 I take a hard hit of the coffee and look out the kitchen window to see Malcolm looking back at me through the thick and tall stems of the flower garden next door. There is no embarrassment in his eyes, only relief.

I stroll out to the road to pick up my morning paper and I pause in envy at the sight of Jan Beck putting three kids on the school bus with yet another younger one in her arms. Lucky lady, I think to myself. Sure, she's got four of them, but they use utensils to eat their food and they use flush toilets.

Me? I've got Malcolm—the Doctor Disgusto of the domestic cat. Talk about tough love.

4

RICH CATS DON'T KNOW HOW TO HAVE FUN

I read in yesterday's paper that an entrepreneur from Oshawa, Ontario, forked over $2,000 cash at a cat show to purchase Felix, a rare hairless Sphinx, which she plans to breed, thus earning a small fortune in stud fees.

Imagine that! We've got more than a million unemployed people in this country, and a lady in Oshawa figures out a way to create a cottage industry based on the services of horny household pets. Why isn't this woman in Ottawa behind a door marked "Ministry of Labour"?

And no offence to the lady, but Felix is one ugly little creature—bald, wrinkled and anaemic. To me, Felix the Sphinx looks like he lost a knock-down, drag-'em-out battle with a cordless Lady Remington. He has a set of ears that look like they were transplanted from a large albino German shepherd who died of acute surprise.

About the only advantages I see to owning a Sphinx like Felix are there are no hairballs to clean up in the spare room

and you don't have to Magic Brush the furniture before company arrives.

But is this worth $2,000, especially when you have to sit in the waiting room at the veterinary clinic and hold a cat that the dogs are uncertain whether to bark at or nurse?

According to the report I read, a Sphinx mysteriously pops up once in a long while in a litter from a union of cats with fur. "A genetic accident" is the way they described it.

"Wait one Wainfleet minute!" I said to myself. When it comes to genetic accidents, I own the Chernobyl of cats. Malcolm owes his life to crooked chromosomes.

And yet I hesitated. What kind of person would parade and prostitute a poor bald cat for the sake of a quick $2,000 profit? It took me almost a full hour to catch Malcolm once he saw me coming with the straight razor and the can of Gillette Foamy. I'll tell you, it was some chase. He spun out around so many corners and skidded sideways so many times, he looked like a candidate for the Domino's Pizza Driver Training School.

I was reeling with excitement. Malcolm isn't worth a nickel with hair, but shaved bald and wrinkled I could get a small fortune for him. This must have been the same strategy Yul Brynner's agent used to land him the lead in *The King and I*.

I got him all foamed up and was just about to start with his whiskers when I looked at the razor and remembered: Many years ago another sharp instrument had sheared off Malcolm's manhood. I could shave him and maybe even sell him, but a spayed stud is like a eunuch opening up a personal chequing account at a sperm bank. You don't get a free pop-up toaster for just filling out the forms. No play, no pay, as they say.

Just to make sure, I called Dr. David Thorne, Malcolm's vet, and asked if the operation he did on Malcolm was reversible. He explained to me that it was not a vasectomy but a castration he had performed. Further discussion revealed my worst fear: the science of modern veterinary medicine had not kept pace with the magical powers of Krazy Glue.

"Besides," said Dr. Thorne, reading from Malcolm's file, "Malcolm's sixteen years old."

"That's nothing," I countered before hanging up. "Pierre Trudeau was in his seventies the last time he fathered a kid."

Life is so unfair.

Here I am stuck with a homely cat with fur who walks funny and does this neat trick where he turns your average indoor flowerpot into a litter box right before the disbelieving eyes of a houseful of guests—and he's not even tax-deductible. On the other hand, the lady from Oshawa has an ugly cat that's so bald he looks like the mascot for Cy Sperling's Hair Club for Men ("remember, Felix is not just the hair club vice-president, he's also a donor"), and he stands to make $5,000 on stud fees and the eventual sale.

There's a big difference between the rich and the poor of cats. For instance, Felix's full name is—and I am not making this up—Les Devon Chat Felix Feneon. On the other hand, Malcolm's full name is Le Chat Qui Gorks Sur La Freakin' Rug Toujours. As you can see, they share aristocratic roots.

Name-calling aside, my interest in narrowing this cultural chasm between Malcolm and the rich cat was piqued enough to actually attend a cat show. I'd never been to a cat show, so I had no idea what to expect.

The show I attended was held at Brock University, in St. Catharines, Ontario. Outside the building I imagined I'd see some pretty mangy-looking dogs milling about, testing the security and scalping tickets, but all I saw were people smoking. I thought for sure I'd see two hell-raisers in peewee hockey jackets, one with a box of mice under his arm, but all I saw was a woman having a sneezing attack. I thought I'd see a gaggle of young feline groupies trying to get photos autographed by the studs being ushered in by their handlers, but all I saw was cat litter spread over patches of ice at the entrance.

Once inside, I stood near the entrance to the gymnasium, absolutely appalled as the cats were formally signed in. I once attended Brock University. Like everyone else, I've heard of the deteriorating state of our education system, but witnessing 282 cats being registered at an accredited Canadian university—well, good Lord! I had no idea university admission standards had dropped so low!

Inside, it wasn't at all what I had imagined. I suppose I was anticipating some sort of beauty pageant for pets—sassy little Siamese with silicon breasts sashaying around hulking male tabbies with pectoral implants. What I saw was a couple of hundred precocious pedigrees being pampered and fawned over like the Roman emperor Caligula.

They are gorgeous animals, almost all of them lolling away their time in plush carpeted cages stretched out in overstuffed round beds and arrogantly ignoring the feathered teasers used to tickle their whiskers. After the opening jitters, the participants settle into a bored exhibition of exhaustion and extravagance, a quiet and orderly affair, interrupted occasionally be the shrieking caterwaul of a contestant who feels he's been lowballed by a biased judge.

And the people! The breeders, owners, trainers, live-in maids and personal appointment secretaries—they are a severely serious bunch, operating in a business of such high finance that a mouse-catcher named Melvin, with healthy hormones, could be worth thousands and thousands of dollars. Serious people like the woman who owns Saint, a strikingly beautiful copper-eyed white Persian worth $2,500. All combed-out and purring, Saint wore a white-and-blue embroidered bib collar and batted big, round eyes at me.

"She's a beauty," I said.

"She's a he," came the curt rebuttal from the owner.

"Dressing him like that, are you not concerned that he may get confused later in life?"

"He's already in stud," she said, pursing her lips.

Oh, that's just great, I thought as I moved on down the line. Saint's highbrow parents will be thrilled when they learn they've raised a cross-dresser.

Unlike at dog shows, I didn't see owners who looked like their cats, but I did see owners who imitated their pets. Like the man who explained to me why he was applying baby powder under the chin of Ragdoll, a fluffy beige Persian.

"He licks himself like this," the man said, sticking his tongue out and down the cleft in his chin. "And then he gets this wet spot down here," he said, cocking his head back and trying to pinpoint the exact area with his tongue, which now seemed even longer than it did the last time it came out.

"Yeah, I know what you mean," I said, trying to sympathize with the man in his grotesque pose. "I've got an uncle in Nova Scotia who does that." Walking away from his blank stare, I was well aware of the difference between his pure-bred Ragdoll and my uncle in Antigonish. My uncle Ranald didn't make $500 every time he successfully mated with a female of his own species.

I was wondering where Malcolm might fit into all this, and I was shocked to learn there wasn't an old-timers' category, something like "Over Fifteen and Up." Much like a professional athlete, Malcolm's age increasingly counts against him in the youthful business of cat shows.

When I met Devon, the fourth-ranked male Chartreuse in North America, I knew Malcolm's chances of getting into a cat show were about the same as me getting a big laugh out of airport security with a really funny bomb joke. Devon, a gorgeous grey-blue specimen owned by Marcus Click of Concord, North Carolina, could be Malcolm's identical twin brother. That is, if living things could be airbrushed.

Technically, most of Malcolm used to be classified as a Russian blue, but according to the World Cat Breeders' International Registry, since the fall of the Berlin Wall he is now officially a French Chartreuse. Similarly, since the first war in Iraq, Elbash Persians have been upgraded to Long Hair Patriots. Believe me, cataclysmic world events cause just as much upheaval in the pet world as they do in the human world. Just ask a penguin in the Falklands or a camel in Baghdad who used to have two humps.

Actually, there wasn't a great deal of difference between Devon the purebred and Malcolm the pauper, except that Devon is 105 human years younger than Malcolm and still has all his body parts. Devon flies all over the continent to win grand prizes at adjudicated exhibitions. Malcolm once went as far as Oakville in my suitcase as I made my way to Pearson International Airport for a trip to England.

That's not to say Devon and Malcolm have nothing in common. Far from it. For instance, Devon, this regal, statuesque creature, is worth about what I paid for my '88 Honda Civic Special, and Malcolm has actually ridden in this car.

The more I saw of this gorgeous creature named Devon and compared him with Malcolm, the more convinced I became that there was some pretty subtle segregation going on here. And sure enough, after carefully reading the rules and regulations of the Cat Fanciers' Association, I came up with the following areas in which they discriminate against cats like my Malcolm:

- Biting the judge is basis for disqualification. (At my house, it's a form of endearment.)

- Cats found to have fleas or parasites are automatically disqualified. (And . . . And there's not even a special achievement award for a cat who manages to have both!)
- Although points are given for shape, size and placement of ears, judges put no value in "notches."
- In considering the pedigree and breeding heritage of show-calibre cats, the association refuses to recognize "one-night stands."
- There is absolutely no reward for amazing cat feats like the 20-metre litter box dash, the three-and-a-half-minute yawn or grinning with just two teeth.
- Cats are judged on eyes that are "rounded and open, alert and expressive." Not one measly point for "closed most of the time."
- They reward cats with "long tails tapering to an oval tip." "Kinks" rate a big fat zero.
- And coats! This galled me the most. They rate a cat's coat according to "wooliness of texture and resiliency." Now don't you think they should offer a door prize for the cat who looks so embarrassed by his coat, he wishes he could run out and buy one off the rack?

No, I'm sorry, but Malcolm will not be submitting his resumé to the Cat Fanciers' Association until they open their membership up to "Strays," "Runts" and "Over 100 and Still Shakin'." When the CFA wakes up and smells the sardines, Malcolm will be on the cover of their monthly magazine as the Grand Triathlon Champion (a three-sport wonder specializing in Tossing the Hairball, Boxing with Deceased Rodents and Mooning Judges Who Deserve It).

And I wouldn't trade the little bugger for the world. Money and a free kitten to be named later, maybe. But the world, no way.

I left the cat show depressed. It wasn't my idea of a real good time. I would have liked to have plopped down on the floor and wrestled a couple of hefty Persians, two falls out of three. I would have loved to have grabbed hold of the microphone and done my famous rabid Rottweiler impersonation for a little comic relief. I would have enjoyed throwing on the soundtrack from *Cats* and getting all 282 felines up on the dance floor at once.

A sign on several of the cages put it all in perspective and, frankly, put me off: "Don't touch me! Your kind affection could spread infection." Sorry, but when it comes to cats, the only papers I respect are the rolled-up ones I hold in my hand when I periodically put Malcolm through his retraining program.

I'd like to be able to say that I went to a cat show and a dog fight broke out. But that would have woken everybody up.

5
LECTURES:
KEEP IT SIMPLE

Although Malcolm did not attend Brock University with the more affluent cats, he was not completely deprived of a formal education! Twice since we've been living together I have had occasion to sit Malcolm down and deliver a solemn and informative lecture. Oddly enough, both situations arose from propagandist statements issued by the White House.

Lecture #1, "Just Say No to Chicken Bones," was precipitated by First Lady Nancy Reagan's slogan designed to wipe out the multibillion-dollar business of illicit drugs coming into the United States. You may recall this brilliant campaign, in which she urged schoolchildren to chant: "Just Say No to Drugs." This program had about the same effect on the drug trade as Colombian coffee had in keeping President Reagan awake during cabinet meetings. But it was catchy and constantly in the news, and one day I had to use it to admonish my little Malcolm.

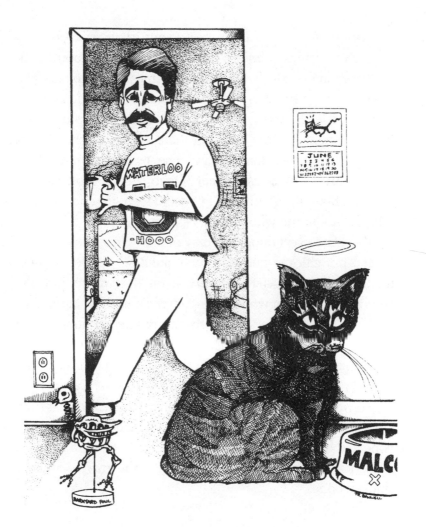

Now you have to understand, my cat goes absolutely mental over chicken bones. Obsessed is this two-toothed cat that irrationally covets the dried and meatless remainder of a dead and dumb fowl. I can wrap them in plastic and put them in a lid-locked garbage pail behind a kid-proof cupboard door, and in the morning there will be chicken bones all over the kitchen floor. But I can never catch him doing it. In the morning he gives me that "Oh my gosh!" look, like the Chicken Bone Burglar broke in again last night and he's just as upset about the whole thing as I am.

I've tried everything, to no avail.

If I put chicken bones in the crankcase of a John Deere tractor chained to a flatbed truck on its way to Lincoln, Nebraska, Malcolm would intercept the shipment at the Fort Erie border—and the next morning my kitchen floor would again look like a bird cemetery.

If Amelia Earhart had taken off in 1937 with chicken bones in her bomber jacket, Malcolm would have located her by now.

So my options were: give up eating chicken or eat only de-boned chicken; disguise a German shepherd as a chicken bone and have him hide in the cupboard; or create a bedtime story that would impress upon Malcolm the grave danger of chicken bones.

So I sat Malcolm down on the bed and pretended to open a book, using two record album covers. (Hey, he's a cat. What does he know about hardback books?"

"Once upon a time," I began this parable, "there was a mama bear and a papa bear. But they weren't really bears, they were a mama and a papa—plural. That is, The Mamas & The Papas."

The lullaby I sang went like this:

> *McGwinn and McGwire just are gettin' higher.*
> *In L.A. you know where that's at.*
> *And no one's gettin' fat 'cept Mama Cass.*

I explained to Malcolm that my generation feared that The Mamas & The Papas would chemically hurt themselves as they did so much dope that the Colombian drug cartel issued them a 1-800 number for ordering.

> *McGwinn and McGwire couldn't get much higher.*
> *But that's what they were aimin' at.*
> *And no one's gettin' fat 'cept Mama Cass.*

I explained to Malcolm how The Mamas & The Papas did so many drugs that they should have been required to list themselves on the New York Stock Exchange as a pharmaceutical research and development corporation.

McGwinn and McGwire are just a-catchin' fire.
In L.A. you know where that's at.
And everybody's gettin' fat 'cept Mama Cass.

Like all good fables mine had a good mix of wisdom and wickedness and I had several proponents on both sides burned at the stake to let Malcolm know I was serious about this lecture.

When I got to the part where I explained the existentialism of "California Dreamin'" and how it wasn't so much a song as a mind-altered state of consciousness that causes a person to order a pizza by phone while forgetting to give a name and address—Malcolm cocked his head in that wonderfully inquisitive way that only cats do, as if to say: "So, what are you saying, Uncle Bill? Are drugs bad?" (Malcolm's going through a parental identity crises and so far I'm ignoring the "Uncle Bill" stuff.) But the cat is a quick read, no doubt about it.

"Well, not necessarily, Malcolm," I said. "Mama Michelle Phillips and Papa John Phillips lived to write best-selling books about the tandem loads of drugs they did back in the sixties. They made millions from their stories.

"Well then, what's the point, Uncle Bill?" he asked.

"The point is, Malcolm," I said patiently, "Mama Cass choked on a chicken bone and died in her bed.

"Just say no to chicken bones," I concluded in a fatherly tone, pulling the covers up around his chin.

Malcolm stared at me for five maybe seven minutes before I realized he was sound asleep with his eyes open. The telling of the tale had taken its toll before the moral of the story could kick in.

But you know, I think it worked. Last night I had chicken for dinner and this morning the bones are still in the garbage. Of course, this afternoon I caught the little beggar with his paw in the medicine chest looking for non-prescription drugs but hey—it's a start.

He eventually gave up his obsession with chicken bones and it would be years before I faced the need to sit him down again for another lecture.

As a matter of fact, the Gulf War might have slipped right by Malcolm unnoticed except for a statement issued by a White House spokesperson. (That's the first war in Iraq, President George Bush Senior's war in Iraq, not George Bush

Junior's war in Iraq. Thank goodness George Junior never had a son.) Of all the propaganda that preceded the war, Malcolm paid particular attention to the phrase "Desert Rats."

Dramatically and uncharacteristically, Malcolm revealed his innermost fear, that he and K.C., the Siamese from three doors down, might be called up to fight in the Persian Gulf. I assured him he had nothing to worry about. At seventeen years of age (119 in human years) he was way too old to be drafted.

(But we both agreed neither one of us would be too upset if they shipped that stupid Siamese over there!)

I should tell you up front that both Malcolm and I were fervently opposed to the Gulf War. In fact, I urged my local member of Parliament to introduce a bill declaring that if the Canadian Navy could not reach the war zone within one calendar year and/or ultimately could not find the Persian Gulf, then the war would be cancelled.

But we both changed our position on the war while watching it on television.

Out here in Wainfleet, cable is the implement used to pull teenaged drivers out of ditches late on Saturday night. Cable television is still a hi-tech rumour, something city folk can order over the telephone.

So Malcolm and I are watching the war on Channel 7's "Eyewitness News," the ABC network signal that comes across the lake from Buffalo quite clear. And early on, news anchor Irv Weinstein reveals that Iraqi President Saddam Hussein is "monitoring troop movements by watching CNN."

CNN!?! Malcolm looked at me with that blank stare of betrayal. *CNN!?!*

We were watching the war on a local network affiliate while Saddam was sitting in his bunker—no doubt sipping a beer and munching popcorn with his feet up on a pile of generals who had disobeyed him that morning—watching CNN.

After all the atrocities—the invasion of Kuwait, the gassing of Kurds, the raping, the pillaging, the shooting of all the animals in the Kuwaiti Zoo (which, by the way, pissed Malcolm off so much he requested that the front pages carrying Saddam's photo be used to line his litter box)—on top of all these heinous crimes we found out the man also has an illegal cable hook-up!

That's when we turned the channel changer on to our anti-war sentiments. The man had gone too far. Saddam had cable and we didn't? That's when we said, let's go in there and rip that infidel's tongue out and feed it to a stray dog.

Confused as I was about a televised war that deployed smart bombs and employed stupid people, I thought I put the matter to rest by explaining to Malcolm about Field Marshal Rommel and his World War Two tank fighters known as Desert Rats. He finally understood they weren't *real* rats.

But as quickly as the issue disappeared, it was back again the next day. Actually, Malcolm brought the topic up after breakfast, which delighted me because if I had to eat what I made him eat, I'd have brought up breakfast.

"So, what's this business about 'the Dogs of War,' Uncle Bill?" he asked, a few bits of gravy matter perched under the opening of each nostril. (He was still cutting me no slack whatsoever on the father/son thing.) His preoccupation with rats and dogs seemed to indicate a very loose grasp of the situation in general and the effect of sanctions in particular.

So down we sat for Lecture #2, "The New World Is Out of Order." With Malcolm on my lap making happy, gurgling noises, I briefed him on international flashpoint crisis management exactly the way President Bush would describe the situation to Vice-President Quayle. Malcolm, too, was drooling a little.

Malcolm was visibly relieved when I explained that "Dogs of War" was a figure of speech referring to the hostile and destructive nature of war rather than to real dogs like, say, Hiseler's German shepherd, who was once responsible for Malcolm spending an entire Labour Day weekend atop a utility pole.

"So, like, who are these 'Dogs of War'?"

"In the Gulf War, I guess the real Dogs of War are Saddam Hussein and George Bush," I replied, as honestly as I could.

I went on to tell him that Saddam Hussein is called "the Butcher of Baghdad"—even though he doesn't own a meat store—which makes him an exceptionally bad person.

"How bad?"

"Well, Malcolm," I explained, "remember the kid who slammed the door on you when you were a kitten, which is why you've always walked funny?"

He nodded reluctantly.

"Well, Saddam Hussein would also have slammed that door on you, causing you permanent disability of the spine, and then he would have ordered you to represent Iraq in the 100-metre sprint at the International Cat Olympics to be held in Brussels in 1994."

Malcolm was horrified. He was certain Cleveland had been awarded those games.

"And George Bush?"

"Well," I said, "he's certainly no dog of . . . I mean, he's not exactly a . . . he's . . . George Bush is no Saddam Hussein!" I concluded.

"Sure," replied Malcolm, "and he's no John Kennedy either!" There were days when you needed passport photos to distinguish Malcolm from Vice-President Quayle.

I went on to draw the analogy that world war breaks out when one male tries to take over another male's territory, like when Irene Kohl's tomcat used to come onto our property to beat the hell out of Malcolm on a daily basis until he was finally repelled by my starter's pistol.

Malcolm didn't remember any specific losses in battle, but he sure remembered Irene Kohl's cat. What I remembered was comparing Malcolm to his dental records to make certain it was him.

"Anyway, one day Saddam Hussein strayed into the territory of Kuwait and he staked out all the borders of Kuwait as his own property," I said.

"Wow!" exclaimed Malcolm. "This guy Hussein must have a bladder the size of New Brunswick!"

Malcolm sometimes mistakenly gives geopolitical analogies a much too literal or personal interpretation. And he's not too good at getting hardened pieces of Mixed Grill out of his nose either, though he kept trying even as we spoke.

No, I explained, Saddam Hussein didn't actually urinate along every inch of Kuwait's 200-mile border with Saudi Arabia. That's stupid. He paid Cuban mercenaries and Soviet advisors to do it.

"So, what's the point, Uncle Bill?"

"Well, Malcolm, you know how when a male comes into your territory you'll fight him, but when a female comes onto the property you both just scream and hiss and howl but there's no fighting?"

"Yeah."

"Well, if we had more women running this world, we wouldn't have war."

He thought about this for a long time and then came back with a series of four questions.

"Yes," I answered, "there would be a lot of hissing and howling but no war.

"No, I don't think you can blame it all on PMS.

"Yes, I'm quite familiar with the term.

"Yes, they'd be late for meetings because the blow-dryer overheated and yes, they'd have to leave early to pick up the kids at daycare, but no war.

"You see, Malcolm, mothers won't send their babies to die in some godforsaken, rinky-dink dustbowl in the middle of nowhere." Malcolm looked hurt. I'd forgotten he'd been orphaned in Welland.

"But I don't get it," he said. "Hussein invaded Kuwait's territory . . . So how come George Bush has to fight him? Does Bush own Kuwait?"

Boy, Art Linkletter was right—cats say the damnedest things!

I was nervous about the conclusion we were both coming to here. "I guess in a sort of non-literal sense, America thinks it does own Kuwait and all the problem areas of the world, at least to the point of securing their territorial borders. The U.S. is the policeman of the new world order."

Malcolm's eyes locked on me like a heat-seeking missile onto a Soviet MiG with a broken air-conditioner. What followed was a "movie moment," a mental collision of heightened awareness and suspended disbelief as Malcolm and I looked into each other's eyes and, as if rehearsed, said simultaneously: "Wow! George Bush is going to need a bladder the size of Texas!"

And we never had another lecture. The results were starting to scare us both.

6
PET FOOD
PEOPLE

Lecturing Malcolm was one thing. Lecturing a group of people, I found out, could be hazardous to your health.

If someone had ever suggested I would be asked to formally speak to a group on behalf of Malcolm, I would have formally requested that that person be drug-tested. On the other hand, I could certainly see myself speaking on behalf of Malcolm in a court of law.

"Your Honour, I realize all my neighbours' houses have been broken into and items of food have been removed. I'm just saying I've never seen Malcolm in possession of burglar tools."

"Yes, your Honour, I agree it looks rather suspicious that all the empty food containers were found under my bed, but ah, you know, maybe he bought them on the street and didn't know they were stolen goods."

"Yes, I realize we're talking truckloads here, but I assure you all that food was strictly for his own personal use. No, he was not dealing."

"Well, yes, your Honour, as a matter of fact, a cooked ham *is* just a snack for this cat."

As a defence witness certainly, but as a guest speaker, or more precisely a ghost speaker, for Malcolm—hardly.

Nonetheless, word got out that Malcolm loved Miss Mew, and the cat food manufacturer started sending him free samples, placemats and dishware. Next came a request

for me to speak at a national convention of pet food people at a big hotel in Toronto.

The whole event was based on a false premise. The pet food people thought Malcolm loved Miss Mew cat food. Not a chance. The cat food he tolerated; it was Miss Mew he loved! In fact, he tried to book himself into the hotel's honeymoon suite in the hope that she might show up at the convention. I can't tell you the number of times I caught Malcolm under the bedsheets with a flashlight and a label with Miss Mew's picture on it.

During lunch I scanned the pet food audience, trying to get a feel for this group. They were subdued, but that really wasn't the word I was looking for. They were serene, but that didn't tell the whole story either. This group was modestly restrained, no, unostentatious with a communal sense of silence, but no . . . Moments before I was introduced I realized this group was deceased. Yeah, that's the only word for it—*deceased*.

According to the information of the agenda, many of these people had spent twenty-two years in the pet food industry. They must have seen a lot of changes. I mean, twenty-two years ago the accepted definition of pet food was a live rodent who just wasn't paying attention.

From my first moments onstage I realized that having a drink at lunch was strictly forbidden by this group and that laughter had also been outlawed in the charter of their organization. This was a group bent on having a miserable time, and the feeling was that my presence assured them of achieving this goal.

I must tell you, it was not my fault. Ultimately I would blame Malcolm for getting me into this mess, but at the time I believe I gave them some pretty good ideas on how to improve their business.

For instance, the pet food people market a "pet food palatability enhancer," a white powder you mix with your pet's food to make it more attractive. The problem is, pets take one look at the canned stuff and think they're part of a recycling program. Why would they eat it twice?

So I made mention of their pet food palatability enhancer and said it was a shame they hadn't developed a palatability enhancer for people food twelve years earlier, otherwise I might still be married.

Ha, ha, ha, ha, ha, ha, ha, ha.

That was me laughing. They were busy cleaning their fingernails.

But did I quit? No.

I suggested to these people that if the statistic I had read was correct, that if there really were going to be 9.5 million canines in Canada by 1995, then maybe they should be developing condoms for dogs or sidewalks that flush.

Ha, ha, ha, ha, ha, ha, ha.

That was me laughing again. The pet food people were all stifling yawns in unison. That line had doubled Malcolm up when I tried it on him in rehearsal.

But did I quit? Of course not. That would've been prudent.

So I said to these people, these designers of pet products, that if all cats were like my little Malcolm maybe they should be working on a pet food that's 40 percent tuna and 60 percent Lavoris.

Ha, Ha.

Yeah, me again. The pet food people were all shifting uncomfortably in their seats. I had left that one out of the rehearsal.

But did I quit? Does Seafood Supreme taste anything like it sounds?

So I hit 'em with my best shot. I said to these people, this still life billboard of pained and painted faces—I said, you know, what you need to do is create a chain of fast-food restaurants and spaying clinics for pets. Think of it, I said, feed 'em and fix 'em in under four minutes, and you could call the place McNeuters!

Ha, ha—clunk!

That was me laughing and knocking my water glass off the lectern. The audience was flicking bits of lint off their trousers and skirts. I must admit, Malcolm, too, had been squeamish about that one.

Silence. Deep, ear-splitting silence. As my uncle Ranald from Antigonish used to say, "You could hear an ant piss on a pillow three blocks away."

Folks, if rock-bottom counts, I was a hit.

As I stepped down off the podium I noticed all the catering staff were wearing black armbands and dabbling at their eyes with hankies. The pet food people were nodding off as one. Somebody nicknamed a guy in the back who had snored through my entire address "Lucky."

Before I left I told them all in no uncertain terms that I'd had it, I was boycotting pet food forever. And I meant it, too. Oh, I'll still buy it for Malcolm, but I'll never eat another tin of that stuff as long as I live.

On the drive back to Wainfleet I spotted a bumper sticker that asked "Where Will You Spend Eternity?" As I passed the car I mouthed to the driver: "Been there."

Sometimes late at night, all of a sudden the wind will stop howling and the house will quit creaking and there'll be this gaping hole of silence in the air. Quickly, I'll sit up and tell a funny pet food story, and sure enough the silence gets heavier and more profound—and I know it's the applause of the pet food people. These people will haunt me forever.

On the bright side, Malcolm never tires of that joke about dogs and condoms and sidewalks that flush.

7
MALCOLM
THE POSTER BOY

Although Malcolm's star status took a plunge at the pet food convention, it appeared to peak one year later.

In 1989 Canada's first naturalized terrorist scored very low marks for vehicle selection when he hijacked a bus and it got stuck in the mud on Parliament Hill. The fact that nobody could read his handwriting when he delivered a list of his demands also helped to jeopardize his project.

In 1989 *Jesus of Montreal* won big at Cannes, and Canada was still smarting from Ben Johnson's gold medal fiasco at the Seoul Olympics. The speed with which he went from being Canada's own Ben Johnson to Jamaican-born Ben Johnson even impressed his sprint coach Charlie Francis.

And in 1989, the Humane Society of Welland, Ontario, named Malcolm Thomas their Cat of the Year. The directors who made this decision are by all accounts reasonable people who are all allowed to vote and operate motorized vehicles.

It must be pointed out that Malcolm did not apply or in any way campaign for the title. Many times he vowed that if nominated he would not stand, if elected he would not attend the parade.

Malcolm was fourteen at the time—wobbly when walking and irritating when talking. He could not climb a tree, catch a mouse, or clean his whiskers without getting a claw caught in a nostril. And here he was becoming famous.

I wrote the columns, I did the speaking engagements, I brought home the bacon, and yet I couldn't write a cheque at the Belmont Hotel without first producing two pieces of photo I.D.

I now know what drove Desi Arnaz to drink.

Malcolm's celebrity status began that year when a class at Glynn A. Green Public School, in Fonthill, requested a personal appearance and, much to the disappointment of all concerned, I showed up. They wanted Malcolm.

The class had sent him thirty-two personal letters asking questions such as how would he bring about world peace and suggesting depraved, albeit original ways in which he could drive me even further over the brink.

When one little girl requested a photograph I blushed and said I really didn't have any photos of myself. She got a round of laughs when she replied, "Not you, silly—da cat!"

They were great kids, and I'm sure I'll meet them again someday if I'm ever asked to cut the ribbon at a juvenile detention centre.

Pretty soon requests were received at newspapers carrying my weekly column to replace my photo with Malcolm's. Although at least half these letters could be traced directly back to my mother, the number was still significant.

Malcolm's new-found fame seemed to hairball—sorry, snowball—soon after that.

When I wrote a column about Malcolm being sick, get-well cards poured in, and a lovely lady, Mrs. Medvic, the wife of Wainfleet's water man, showed up at my door with fresh homegrown catnip and a sure-cure recipe.

Reader Claire Sametz of Fort Erie began clipping columns on Malcolm and sending them to her niece JoJo, a dealer in Las Vegas, who in turn passed them on to fellow blackjack dealers. Malcolm started getting postcards from Las Vegas, where he became nearly as big a deal as Wayne Newton's boxer shorts.

And so it was that the Welland Humane Society named Malcolm their 1989 Poster Boy and produced a line of calendars, buttons and bumper stickers in his name. The purpose of the campaign was to promote pet adoptions. I thought this was great. I figured if the program really took off I could find a good home for Malcolm. I misunderstood.

The plan was fairly simple: get a family photograph of Malcolm and me, and the Humane Society would have it reproduced on calendars above a caption line "Feeling Way Too Happy? Adopt This Cat" or "Free to a Good Home—The One Without the Moustache" or "Take the One Who Has All His Shots."

It sounded pretty straightforward. Problem was, somebody forgot to get a contractual consent form for the whole campaign with Malcolm's pawprint at the bottom.

Archie Hood, Welland's finest photographer, called and we set up a picture-taking session at my place. I had no idea Malcolm enjoyed having his picture taken about as much as actor Sean Penn.

Archie arrived with tripods, light meters, eight lenses, three cameras, two flashes and one sun reflector. As it turned out, he had brought everything except what we really needed: a professional cat wrangler.

The first setting Archie chose was my office desk, and we thought it would be cute if Malcolm had his paws on the keys of the typewriter and I'd be looking over his shoulder anxiously anticipating his every word. Never mind that I had to borrow a typewriter because I don't own one and Malcolm is an atrocious speller—hey! this is show business.

So everything is set—camera, lights, action—and I yell for Malcolm, who, whenever I've done this, has faithfully come running and jumped into my lap each and every day since he was a kitten, yet this time the little scamp runs full tilt past my office and into the bedroom, where he dives behind the headboard, all the while making hideous threatening noises as if he's been gargling with laughing gas. Archie managed to get a great shot of me down on all fours beside my bed with the liver pâté in one hand and a noose in the other.

Once back at the desk, Archie took a quick series of a dozen photos, all showing me holding Malcolm in a half nelson and him glaring and hissing at anything that moved. The typewriter sits idly in the background. One of these photos was actually used for the Humane Society calendar, and if you ever see it, you'll notice my right wrist is cut and bleeding. It's the first time I can recall that a domestic cat may have been seriously considered for a guest appearance on Marlin Perkins' "Mutual of Omaha's Wild Kingdom."

We tried a variety of other locations—by the fireplace, on the grass by the horseshoe pits, down on the beach—all with varying degrees of failure. But Archie, like all great photographers who will spend an entire day trying to get that one unique shot in which the subject (me) may actually get killed on camera, wanted one more set-up.

So we went to a nearby field, and by this time Malcolm is behaving much better mainly because we have him in leg irons and handcuffs. This shot called for me to sit on a boulder with Malcolm in my lap and weeds and trees in the background and the lake off to one side. Both of us would be dreamily staring out across the lake because, by this time, both of us would have preferred to be over there in Dunkirk, New York. In separate bars.

So I've got Malcolm secured to my lap and Archie starts shooting at a rapid-fire pace, and I must say, it was going surprisingly well. That is, until Archie spotted a slight imperfection. Archie immediately stopped shooting and walked toward me ever so reluctantly, and informed me the photo session was over and this last series of photos probably could not be used because of the "water spot."

I thought he said "water spout" and when I wheeled around to look at the lake behind me, Malcolm seized the opportunity to bolt from my lap to under a nearby shed, not to return until nightfall. When I saw Archie staring at my crotch and laughing like a loon, I stood up—and I realized the origin of the "water spot."

That's right, folks, when hissing didn't work and drawing blood had no effect, Malcolm resorted to one of his last strategic weapons—and peed all over my jeans. I'm not saying I didn't deserve it, but it was still a pretty rude thing to do, even for a celebrity. Sean Penn had punched people for trying to get his photograph, but . . .

I never asked about the possibility of airbrushing my crotch, and Archie, ever the gentleman, never mentioned it.

I was thankful for one thing—that Malcolm ran under that shed where we couldn't get him, thus eliminating any possibility of Archie requesting yet another set-up. One more shot may have forced Malcolm to exercise his nuclear option.

That summer I trucked Malcolm around to country fairs, fulfilling his role as the Welland Humane Society's Cat of the Year. Inevitably, kids would come up to the booth and rattle his cage, and the conversation would go like this:

"Doesn't he do tricks or nothing'?"

"No."

"He looks mad."

"He is."

"Why's he here?"

"I have no idea."

"Why are you wearin' that plastic apron?"

"You don't want to know."

When word got around about what Malcolm had done to his owner/handler/publicist in the photo session by the lake, no agent would touch him and his fame remained rather local. Looking back, I think it was a conscious decision. Every celebrity at some point has to decide whether to remain a big fish in a small pond or become a small fish in a big pond. Malcolm clearly chose to remain a big cat in a small litter box.

Oddly enough, the "water spot" incident did a lot for my career, and I received hundreds of letters from readers. And I kept them all, too. I just cut out the part where they said, "I've been wanting to do that to your column for years!"

Ah, fame, so fleeting, so illusive. But if you scrub real hard, it will come out with bleach.

8
STILL WEIRD AFTER
ALL THESE YEARS

I don't know if the thirteenth year of a cat's life coincides with the feline change of life, but it was right around that time that Malcolm developed some pretty peculiar habits. More peculiar even than using my lap as a travelling commode. Maybe it was just a case of the bored leading the jaded, but somebody in this story had way too much on his paws.

I don't know exactly how or when this thing got started, but somewhere around the ninth day in a row that I found Malcolm staring at a hole in the ground, I suspected there might be a problem.

Not long ago I was returning home from the Becks', where I had delivered a perfectly good hornet's nest that high winds had blown out of a tree in my front lawn. I reckoned the kids would take it to school and have fun with it, playing show-and-tell or sting-and-sing or let's-jam-this-up-Mrs. Conigg's-tailpipe.

Anyway, that's when I saw Malcolm hunched down in the grass, his paws tucked in under his chest, his overbite fixed in a stupid grin, and staring straight down into this hole. The hole was about three inches in diameter in high grass, three cottages to the east of me.

I left him alone. Nearing his thirteenth birthday, Malcolm is still looking for his first fresh kill. To my knowledge he has never caught a rodent that wasn't already wounded or in an advanced stage of arthritis. Malcolm considers it a good catch if, when I brush the cobwebs from his whiskers, they contain something that's still moving.

He failed to show up for lunch, so I went over to the hole, picked him up and carried him home.

At supper he failed to respond to the sound of the electric can opener, which is like a boxer failing to answer the bell. This was serious stuff. I went to the hole and carried him home to dinner.

When he wasn't home at eleven-thirty to watch David Letterman and Stupid Pet Tricks (Malcolm thinks they're fixed!), I set out with a flashlight to find him. The beam from the flashlight did not pick up two fluorescent orbs in the night, so my first thought was that he wasn't there. Closer inspection revealed he was in fact there, he was just asleep at the hole.

I shone the light down the hole, and when no eyes shone back, we went home to bed.

The next day was more of the same: Malcolm impersonating a government employee asleep at the switch and me shuttling him between hole and home under my arm like a loaf of bread.

After a while *I* became curious. There had to be something down that hole. Cats may be crazy, but they're far from stupid. I mean, how many humans do you know who have figured out a way to get two square meals a day and their stomachs scratched for doing nothing all day? (Okay, but prisoners and members of Parliament don't count.)

Now there's two of us looking down this hole, and when you sit for a long time lost in contemplation, it's downright frightening, the strange thoughts that come creeping into your mind.

My first thought was that "boa watching" was spreading. Recently, the entire city of Hamilton had spent three days riveted to their television sets while the camera filmed down a toilet pipe in an apartment building where a boa constrictor had last been seen heading south. They were fascinated by looking down this dark hole in a bathroom floor, and I think it said something about the level of civic boredom in that town. It was at that point that the rest of the country realized how very badly Hamilton needs professional hockey. I laughed at the time, but now here I sat three months later keeping vigil over a hole in the ground with a cat that kept nodding off during the exciting parts.

A daydream ripple moved across my brain scan. It may have been self-hypnosis or a form of odd osmosis but, whatever it was, I began to see things in that hole.

First, I saw the Leafs' chances for a Stanley Cup championship running neck-and-neck with Stockwell Day's political future.

There were wide paisley ties down there, and miniskirts, and Bermuda shorts with knee-high socks. There was a well-worn Nehru jacket with Pierre Elliot Trudeau's initials sewn over the front pocket.

There was a lot of mail down there, legibly addressed, properly stamped and marked "Canada Priority Post".

There was a book entitled *The One-Minute Manager*, the story about Joe Clark's term as prime minister. Another book, *Ethics in Federal Politics*, was still shrink-wrapped.

There was a ton of tuna in the hole marked "Grade A" which had been crossed out and re-marked "Third World" which had been crossed out and re-marked "Cat Food" which had been crossed out and re-marked "Deep Six" signed "John Fraser, former minister of fisheries and as a result of this fiasco now Speaker of the House."

There was a booklet addressed to Brian Mulroney's cabinet ministers: "Killing Time While Doing Time."

There was a stack of freshly laundered shirts, large shirts, starched and folded and marked "Pick Up Tuesday—Jimmy Hoffa."

It turns out there really was a boa constrictor in that hole, a dead one with a big grin and a tag on his tail that read "Show business was my life."

There was an owner's manual for a car call the Bricklin, but all the pages were blank.

There was my Sunshine bicycle, some Cub Scout badges and my Omega Delta Sigma fraternity sweater. There was a whole slew of mementos of my youth, but when my lucky rabbit's foot appeared, Malcolm became quite agitated, and I picked him up and brought him home. I went back when he was asleep and rolled a rock over the hole.

Some things are not meant to be looked into.

I kept him inside for the next while to keep an eye on him, but then Malcolm seemed to develop an indoor abnormality. Watching his coy and curious behaviour ignited an inquisitive glow within my soul and triggered yet another philosophical, almost metaphysical musing: "Hey, how can a cat eleven inches high miss a litter box three feet long?"

According to basic aerodynamic principles, the odds on this happening more than once in a lifetime are infinitely long, like the chances of Canadian unity in our lifetime. The odds of correcting such aberrant behaviour patterns—Malcolm overshooting the end of the litter box and Canadians getting along with each other—are, at best, a long shot. Like Bill Clinton admitting he did inhale and Kim Campbell admitting she couldn't inhale because she couldn't get the joint and her foot in her mouth at the same time.

After years in the sport of litter boxing, I still had my work cut out for me. I have become that naturally dumped-on guy, the reigning champion "quicker-picker-upper." I have no illusions about my talent to train. I suspect that if I could teach Malcolm to do his business in the great outdoors, he'd somehow manage to miss that, too.

Malcolm can drag a three-pound dead catfish from the beach, up fifteen feet of metal stairs, over a three-foot break-wall and across the lawn to the patio, where he then recreates the death scene before the cameras of *Lake Erie's Most Wanted* while neighbours pull up lawn chairs, drink beer and applaud. But the cat cannot master the same body function an amoeba learns at birth.

Malcolm can squeeze through the latched door of a storage shed and haul out a bag of stinking clam shells, thus attracting raccoons from as far away as Port Dover for an all-night seafood and sex festival. But he can't surrender to the force of gravity and just drop things in their proper place.

Malcolm can eat an entire bowl of my chicken noodle soup in less time than it takes me to get up from the couch and tell a carpet-cleaning salesperson on the phone that there is no lady of the house, there are no carpets in the house, there is no house—I live in a car and she's reached me on my cellular. But suddenly he could not, even accidentally, hit the litter box twice in a row.

At first I thought it might be his eyesight, but I felt foolish taking him down to Dr. Thorne and getting him fitted for bifocals, ostensibly to improve his aim at the other end. I tried mounting a rear-view mirror on his front paw—one that warns "Objects In Mirror Are Closer Than They Appear"— but it acted as an anchor and then he never made it to the box at all.

I thought he might hate the clothes dryer that takes the brunt of his bad aim, but when I switched things around in the back hall, he classically soiled a case of John Labatt just the same.

I tried videotaping a litter box session, hoping to review the game film with Malcolm, pointing out the weakness of him as the quarterback not hitting his primary receiver. But unlike Roseanne Arnold, Malcolm won't do rude things on camera.

And then I remembered a problem-solving seminar I'd once attended that suggested when a situation looks impossible look at it from the other side. "Making lemonade out of a lemon" was the quoted cliché.

Yes, I asked myself, what possible positive reinforcement could come from Malcolm overshooting his litter box and hitting the enamel finish of an innocent clothes dryer? Never mind reversing the behaviour. How could I gain some measure of satisfaction from the badly miscalculated results such as they are?

Well, when I mulled over the words *badly miscalculated*, the problem was solved there and then.

I rushed down to my local M.P.'s office and received a four-colour photograph of our smiling prime minister, Mr. Badly Miscalculated. Then I got out the masking tape and, using the clothes dryer as a backing, I . . . I gave Malcolm a framed, four-colour purpose in life.

Suddenly I understand the art of deal-making and compromising and rolling with the dice. Now Malcolm has a goal to shoot for and I don't so much mind when he misses. It's kind of a match made in heaven but played out in the litter box.

I felt so good about Malcolm expressing the kind of appreciation for our prime minister that many of us felt but could not bring ourselves to demonstrate, that I called for a celebration.

I decided to throw Malcolm a dinner party since it was his birthday, but the mere mention of eating triggered another one of those profound musings that had been tormenting me: "Hey, how can a cat two hands tall splash food four feet up a wall?" This question is driving me up said wall and clear around Ramey's Bend. It has become increasingly clear to me that when Sir Isaac Newton founded the theory of universal gravitation, he had not visited Wainfleet to see my Malcolm eat.

Watching Malcolm go at his food is a memorable experience. It's like the first time you saw the shark crunch a swimmer in half in *Jaws*. It's like a food fight in a John Candy movie. It's like the last time you'll ever eat meatloaf in your life.

When the lady next door comes in to feed him while I'm away, her husband always cautions her before she leaves their house: "Don't get hurt, honey. Don't get between him and the bowl."

Until I saw Malcolm eat, the most disgusting sight I'd ever seen was a one-year-old left alone in a highchair with a jar of mashed bananas. Now, after putting a bowl of warm smelly glop in front of him for the 10,260th time, I could watch a whole team of tiny tots share a plate of creamed corn and strained carrots and I probably wouldn't gag. If nothing else, watching Malcolm eat has given me the courage to again stand in line for the buffet at the Belmont Hotel.

So, his birthday bash was much of the same, except we ate at the dining-room table with party favours and candles.

Malcolm's a little sensitive lately about what's going down the chute because he's got an inflammation of the gums called eosinophilic ulcer. That's the expert's opinion. Personally, I think it's just skid marks left by food particles trying to escape the holocaust.

After Dr. Thorne informed me of the ulcer, he told me I better sit down for the next prognosis: judging from Malcolm's heartbeat and appetite, he'll probably live to torment me for another thirteen years.

So, one of us had something to celebrate—break out the New Brunswick sardines but hold the Tabasco.

It was great. I sang "Happy Birthday" and he put his paws over his ears; I sprinkled catnip in an empty cardboard box and he flipped out watching me roll around in it.

It was a perfect party. Right up until Malcolm started eating the candles. And when I dove across the table to keep his fur from getting singed, his party hat caught on fire. God, I hate when that happens.

9

CHRISTMAS~ WE BOTH SHOULD BE IN A HOME FOR THE HOLIDAYS

Truthfully, I'd rather attend a birthday party with my hat on fire than face Christmas. I hate Christmas. Definitely, 'tis not my season to be jolly.

Why, you ask, could anybody hate Christmas when we've moved substantially closer to peace on earth now that Communism is dead and Imelda Marcos's bulletproof bra has been returned to her by the Philippine government? (Do you realize her squad of shoeshine boys outnumbers the Philippine army?!?) Still, there are a lot of things that depress me at this time of year.

First, they always release another Zamfir Christmas album, which I think just adds to the workload of people who staff suicide hot-lines.

Then there's always that highly improbable story about the virgin in the manger giving birth to the kid with no father. Folks, I grew up in a rural hamlet called Dain City. If I've heard that story once, I've heard it a hundred times: "But we didn't even do it!" The only difference is that in Bethlehem this story resulted in the beginning of Christianity, and in Dain City it always ended in a shot-gun wedding. Girls in Dain City could never understand how their parents could believe the Bible but never the boyfriend.

And of course there's the four-page Christmas card list I have but no longer use, the sixty feet of Christmas lights in the attic that stay right there, and the night-after-night round of Christmas parties that I never get invited to. As I said, 'tis not the season of my good cheer.

But the real reason I hate Christmas is that it's a family time of year and, in my case, the one time every year I have to face the fact that my entire immediate live-in family consists of one very short being who has to be deflea'd on a regular basis.

There's something basically sick about a person who looks forward to spending quality holiday time with someone who drinks out of the toilet and can go days with particles of food encrusted under his nose.

Then there's the perennial problem of a gift. Believe it or not, I once designed a whole line of cat gifts, for true pet lovers. Really. The motif was all Malcolm, the motive was revenge. I called our business Toys Я Me and Malcolm. Honest. I billed it as "a designer line of toys and novelty items by Malcolm, the cat who's seen it all and fallen asleep watching it."

Each item was designed to get even with all those people who made money be defiling and defaming cats. I cringe when I hear of a "funny" new cat gimmick that involves a dead or decimated feline. I know the intent is humour, but it's the wackos-in-waiting who are not beyond trying some of this stuff that worry the hell out of me.

So, for real cat lovers everywhere I invented "Barry the Damp Dumb Human Doll." Barry Gottlieb, of Mad Dog Productions in Richmond, Virginia, is the genius who created "Earl the Dead Cat, the Last You'll Ever Need," a morbid and depraved novelty that encouraged the numb-minded to mistreat man's blessed friend. Well, our Barry the Damp Dumb Human was an exact but small replica of Barry Gottlieb, flat like Earl the Dead Cat so that it would lie just below the surface of the litter in the cat box. You could pull up a chair and tip a few cool ones while your cat enthusiastically baptized Barry the Damp Dumb Human. Barry could be machine-washed and then, with great pleasure, hung out to dry.

Next up was a toy tribute to Simon Bond with serious benefits in the field of veterinary medicine. Simon Bond is, of course, the clever devil who published *101 Things to Do with a Dead Cat*, a kind of manual for abusers of helpless felines. Our novelty item was a small, thin but recognizable look-alike of the creative and probably rich Simon Bond. Ours was the one and only Simon Bond Rectal Thermometer. This item, retailing for under ten dollars, came complete with a list of sickness symptoms for cats in a manual entitled *When Kitties Catch a Fever, Insert Simon*. That's right, whenever your cat's not feeling well, Simon goes in to see what the temperature is.

Toys Я Me and Malcolm would produce personalized gifts as well. For instance, if you sent us a recent photograph of one of those morons who has a "Crushed Kitty" slammed and sticking out of the trunk of his car, we would send you a four-coloured poster of this guy drowning in a bowl of Seafood Supreme with Malcolm hunkering down for his first meal of the day. Malcolm at the bowl is like Dr. Strangelove at the button—nothing can survive such imminent devastation.

Yet another poster features "Spike—The Bulldog That Swallowed Garfield." You know the one, with the cat's tail sticking out of the dog's mouth. Our poster would also sell for $14.98, but it showed a nervous and sweating Spike the

Bulldog as Malcolm shoved a fragmentation grenade up Spike's nose and twirled the pin on his trigger toe. This poster carried Malcolm's original pawprint and the caption: "Say You're Sorry Sucker Or You're Sausage!" Beside Spike and barely noticeable, the Simon Bond Rectal Thermometer is registering a record 121 degrees Fahrenheit, and even Simon is wiping his brow with a handkerchief.

There was also a line of feline novelties like a bumper sticker that read "Just Say No to Catnip" and edible underwear for cats made out of dried liver pâté.

I really thought we were on to something. I did. I believed Toys Я Me and Malcolm would make us millionaires and we'd be able to hire a guy to come to the house every day to open tins of food for both of us. Then the economy went into the dumper and Toys Я Me and Malcolm went right in with it.

So it's back to reality and Christmas and cats being so darn hard to buy for. I mean, what do you buy an arthritic cat with a bladder problem? Depends? Okay, but how do you keep them in place? Bungee cords?

Well, it's just not that simple. Malcolm has yearned all his life for just one thing each and every Christmas: a two-year-old female in the advanced stages of reproductive heat. But what if *meow* means *no* and Malcolm fails to get a pre-sex consensual form filled out? I can't handle that kind of responsibility.

I can't get him what I get my mom and my sisters. It's embarrassing enough to see all of them lined up at Bargain Harold's with their gift certificates, not Malcolm, too.

Cologne would be great but they don't make Oil of Red Snapper. Slippers and a robe sounds nice, but it would just be five more things I'd be picking up after him.

One year I bought him one of those expensive cat beds, round with a form-fitting corduroy cushion. Today it's a wine rack in the basement.

I used to buy him all the latest cat toys, but he just let them all run down and he never once replaced the batteries.

Apparently there's a thirty-minute cassette on the market called *Kitty Video* that shows "birds at close range—chirping, fluttering, flying and walking." The purpose, they say, is "to keep bored cats captivated." It's not the kind of hi-tech toy Malcolm deserves. What Malcolm deserves is a dub of the feature film *101 Dalmatians*, dogs at close range—barking, growling, biting, and treeing cats. The purpose? "To keep a bad cat traumatized."

A trip for Malcolm would be a dream gift (my dream, not his). But the single supplement you have to pay for cats travelling alone these days doubles the price of the package. Plus, airlines will not sell you a one-way ticket for a cat on any of their international destinations. I know. I called.

Food is always a favourite with Malcolm, but how long can you keep raw liver under the tree?

Practical gifts for pets and people are usually the best way to go. I thought about getting Malcolm his own cat-operated can opener, but then what useful purpose would I ever again serve in his life?

What Malcolm really needs is one of those automatic doormats like they have at the supermarket. This way, when he wants to go out he just walks up to the door, onto the mat and presto! The door opens and out he goes. Then when he wants to come back in, which happens to be the exact moment he gets out, he steps on the mat outside and presto! He's back in. At which point he always wants to go out again, and then in again, and out and in and out and in and out again and in again until finally he would become disoriented and pass out until late in the spring of next year. And I would have peace on earth for at least a little while.

Then I would adjust the speed on the automatic door ever so slightly so that as he ages and slows down, the opening and closing action of the door would speed up until this

very simple procedure of exiting and entering the house became an exciting and somewhat dangerous sport that would
cause me to pull up a chair and spectate with the aid of fresh
popcorn and cold beer. You'll never see stuff like this on cable.

As it stands now, he's driven me to the point where I'd
like to put the little scamp out without opening the door at all.

With so little time left, I decided that the basic gifts are
best. So I bought him a toenail clipper that also cuts the ends
off of his hand-rolled catnip cigars, a large tin of Carnation
Evaporated Milk and a cigarette lighter that, when turned
upside down, drains all the coloured liquid out so Miss Mew
appears absolutely naked. All he has to do is use a little imag-
ination and he'll understand the true meaning of Christmas—
it's not the gift that counts, it's the thought.

Merry Christmas, Malcolm. I love you. Get off the
counter.

10
ANNUAL VET DAY

Yesterday was Annual Vet Day. This is not the day on which old guys shuffle down Main Street brandishing rows of shiny medals on their blazers to commemorate wars fought so long ago that soldiers with guns were used instead of computers and smart bombs. (I mean, who knew that IBM would someday be a military superpower?)

Annual Vet Day is the one day each year I have to stuff an old guy by the name of Malcolm kicking and screaming into his wicker travelling basket for his yearly medical checkup at Dr. Thorne's Clarence Street Veterinary Clinic and Yapping Academy, in nearby Port Colborne, Ontario.

David Thorne is a model dog doctor and feline physician. People doctors could learn a lot from his cage-side manner, the care he takes with the patients, the concern he has for their owners.

As a matter of fact, David Thorne performed an emergency appendectomy on me several years ago during that doctor's strike we had in Ontario. The operation came off without a hitch, and you can hardly see the scar today. It was the recovery that damn near killed me. For three days I was all hunched over in one of those cages next to a springer spaniel coming off a tail amputation. Bark and whine, hoot and holler—I nearly drove the poor little guy crazy.

Okay, okay, so I made that story up. But David Thorne really is a great pet doctor.

Malcolm has a healthy hate for doctors who (and he has a point here) routinely and sometimes roughly examine one's private parts without consent, "Like I'm some kind of animal," he'll scream, as I lock the door on his travel cage and secure it with a bungee cord.

On the drive to the clinic I contemplate the distinct difference in the goals humans and pets set for themselves as they shuffle down the rickety stairway of life.

For instance, at sixty-five years of age, Canadians want to cut back on work and accelerate their social, recreational and travel endeavours. At seventy-five they're more inclined to read about life or attempt to write their memoirs. And of course at eighty-five and ninety-five they begin to prepare for the worst—a career in the Canadian Senate.

On the other hand, cats like Malcolm at 119 years of age would really rather be napping. In fact, combining the two natural gifts the Cat God gave him, Malcolm would seriously like to figure out a way to nap and eat at the same time and thereby eliminate *the exhaustive standing-up-and-stretching stage*.

Nonetheless, he has somehow managed to make it to the age of seventeen, appears healthy as a horse and for the most part shows no sign whatsoever of making me a free and happy man.

Malcolm and I have certain secrets to this health and longevity, and I started to mentally tick each off as we made our way along Lakeshore Road on Annual Vet Day.

Eating Habits: As far as I can determine, polyester, glass and living creatures larger than himself are the only things Malcolm will not eat. As much as possible I try to limit his daily intake to one tin of really disgusting foodlike mush such as Beef Buffet and Liver Delight. Time permitting, I will always attempt to open the tin before he eats it. Keep young children and older people well away from the actual event. If you think being under a tree during a lightning storm is a dangerous place to be, try standing between Malcolm and his breakfast.

Teeth Care: Brushing and polishing teeth is now recommended by veterinarians for strong, healthy teeth. If your cat is like my Malcolm and time permits, do both teeth.

Medication: From my experience two adult-strength Tylenol tablets crushed and dissolved in warm milk will sometimes ease physical pain and avert emotional trauma. If this does not work, put him outside, lock the door and get right into the Scotch.

Pilling Your Cat: Administering a pill to your pet can be a very painful experience unless, like me, you buy yourself a pair of those welder's gloves with the cuffs that go right up to your armpits. Gently but firmly open cat's mouth by placing hand over snout and thumb and fingers behind his gums. With other hand, separate jaws and show him a medium-sized wind-up cat toy. Tell him if he spits out that damn pill one more time, the toy goes in next. Place pill as far back in the mouth as possible and hold cat's mouth shut until he swallows it, which if he's like Malcolm will be about the middle of the following week.

Slivers, Tacks and Other Sharp Objects in the Paws: As much as possible I try to carefully hide such items behind doors and curtains where he least expects to step on them. Just kidding.

First Aid: When applying a splint to either the front or hind leg, place wooden support strips on each side of leg and wrap tightly with surgical gauze or 3M Magic Tape. *Note*:

such a procedure is done solely for entertainment and big laughs when friends drop in. If your pet is actually injured or limping, take him to the vet.

Flea and Tick Protection: Create a quiet and intimate atmosphere in which the fleas and ticks can get a good look at the body of the cat they are about to invade and inhabit. This pretty much works for us.

Fever: Sometimes a cat will overheat because of dehydration or extreme excitement or exertion. If you don't have time to take him to the vet, sometimes just showing him the thermometer will reduce his body temperature to the normal level because cats have very good memories.

When Should You Call Your Veterinarian? Frequent urination? Spraying? Abnormal breathing? Persistent coughing or wheezing? Bad breath? Hell, if he's in that bad shape I'd seriously consider calling another veterinarian!

So we enter the waiting room at the clinic with our mental checklist intact, and Malcolm is circling inside his carrying case, working himself into a foul mood, when he spots Bucky, a sad-eyed old beagle looking like rabbits have tormented him every day of his life.

Bucky looks suspiciously at Malcolm as though he might be a big rabbit disguised as a cat and sent here by the boys out back of his house to yet again make a fool of ol' Buck. The tired eyes and the grey around the snout say it all: "Through the bush . . . into the brier . . . around the trees . . . stop at the ditch . . . I'm getting too old for that nonsense." Bucky makes a mental note to attack Malcolm at some unspecified later date and he goes back to scratching himself.

I love watching dogs at the vet's. They all sit there on their very best behaviour and then one will bark and the whole damn works of them chime in like they're the opening act for an Up With People concert. And have you noticed that dogs don't attack cats in the waiting room of veterinary offices? I think maybe a dog will attack a cat on his first visit and then once he experiences the Standard Temperature-Taking Procedure in the examination room, he assumes this is his punishment for what he did to the cat and he never does it again.

In fact, dogs are so civil in veterinary waiting rooms that hunting dogs won't actually point, they'll just clear their throats and nod.

When it's their turn to go in, Bucky and his owner seem to have the routine down pat. The owner stands, jerks Bucky's leash and says, "C'mon boy, let's go." Bucky automatically digs his nails into the tiled floor, stiffens all four legs like boards, and the owner pulls Bucky into the examination room like he's a ceramic lawn ornament.

"Like we're nothing but animals," Malcolm hisses as they close the door behind Bucky, thus eliminating any potential witnesses to the personal body probe that's about to begin.

Then it's our turn.

And Malcolm comes out of his travel hamper much like Bucky left the waiting room—involuntarily. I have him by the scruff of the neck, but then he's got me by the wrist. He locks his claws into the top of the cage, so I turn it upside down. I pull, he hisses. I push, he scratches. Luckily nobody witnesses these events, otherwise they'd have thought we were recently married.

I finally get him out and unwrap him from his favourite blanket. I daub at my bleeding wrist with a Kleenex and naturally the first thing I do is pat him on the head and say, "That's a good boy." At home, that kind of nonsense would earn him a whack that would make his eyes cross, but here at the clinic on Annual Vet Day it's somehow acceptable social behaviour.

I formally introduced Malcolm to David Thorne's new assistant, a dedicated young veterinarian by the name of Theresa deGelder. Malcolm was so impressed he promptly offered up a little sample without her having to ask for it.

That's right, after (and you gotta hand it to him, he predicted this would happen) she probed his innards, pulled his groin area and looked into recesses the average person on the street would have no interest in, Malcolm, in technical veterinarian language, dropped one off the end of the table. He did it so casually, I had trouble believing he was even involved.

As Theresa and I simultaneously looked down at the mess on the floor and then up at each other, my response was swift and honest: "Hey, I didn't do it."

I remember Malcolm had done the same thing years ago to a vet who was way too joyous over the event for my liking. "Oh, look," he said, "Malcolm left a little present on the floor." I couldn't help thinking that this guy must be the easiest person in the world to buy for at Christmas time.

Awkwardness prevailed, I offered to clean it up, but Theresa was already ripping off paper towels and claiming it was all part of the job.

This ugly situation was lightened by the timely bit of comic relief—The Teeth-Checking Procedure.

"Oh, he doesn't have many left, does he?" she observed.

Malcolm was not amused. He gave her the look that said: "For this she studied for seven years at the University of Guelph?"

If I had teeth, he thought, Mr. Tough Guy here wouldn't have fingers.

Anyway, the rest of the examination went smoothly. Even when Theresa shot a syringe full of vaccine into Malcolm's rear end, he never moved a muscle. I guess when you've made your statement on the state of pet care and a paid professional has to address that statement on bended knee with paper towels—well, I guess you've pretty much said it all.

Another fight breaks out when I have to put him back in the travel hamper, much like the one that breaks out at home when I have to get him out again.

Normally, tearing my skin, hissing, growling and spitting at me would earn Malcolm a trip up the backyard flag pole wrapped in the Red Maple Leaf. But today, on Annual Vet Day, what does he get? "A widdle bowl of cold milk because he's such a good boy."

Any way you look at it, folks, a true pet lover is one sick puppy.

11
A GOOD NIGHT'S SLEEP

Somehow and suddenly, Malcolm has gone deaf.

I think it's a direct result of a traumatic shock—probably on Annual Vet Day, the day he met his new veterinarian. Theresa deGelder. Malcolm wasn't paying much attention when I made the introduction. No doubt he was too busy marvelling at the framed wall poster illustrating canine venereal disease and snickering away to himself when suddenly he caught her last name.

"The gelder," he thought. "Good God, not again!"

The thought of somebody taking a scalpel to what little remains of his manhood sent off a siren of terror inside his head, and I believe it deafened him on the spot. Actually, it deafened him on the table upon which he then made a spot.

Yes, and I can back him up on this one, you don't mess with a lady named deGelder. Even the men who bring their pets into the clinic keep their backs to the wall when Theresa's in the room.

So I called Theresa and asked her what could be done about this problem of deafness. You have to understand that Theresa deGelder is a great vet, a straight shooter who does not beat around the bush.

"You can't do a thing," she said. "It's old age. Things stiffen up inside and they just don't work anymore."

"Huh?" I said. I don't know where she gets off talking about me like that. I was inquiring on behalf of my cat . . . and if she had continued by giving me advice on regularity and liver spots, I swear, I would have had to hang up the phone.

I guess I have to face the fact: Malcolm's ears don't work anymore. I love every notch and scar on those pointy little appendages, but it seems they're only there as ornaments from here on in.

Someone told me there are hearing aids for pets, and I looked at a few but they weren't the kind I want. I want the kind that fit into reading glasses. The way I see it, if I'm going to shell out a hundred dollars, I want some entertainment value for my money.

There are certain advantages and disadvantages to Malcolm's hearing loss. The bad part is, he can't hear me calling. The good part is, he can't hear me coming.

I can get down on all fours and follow the little waif all over the house and he has no idea I'm right behind him. Then, by slamming both hands down hard on each side of him, I can send Malcolm three feet straight up in the air, still in a standing position. (Warning to children: Please do not try this at home with your cat. Remember, in any trick that involves the physical propulsion of a household pet, I *am* a professional.)

It's incredible! And the best part is, like all elderly people, he refuses to admit he's gone deaf. Instead, he thinks I've become invisible.

For us, deafness has become a matter of trade-offs. On the one hand, Malcolm can't hear the fridge door open anymore, so I don't have to share my snacks. On the other hand, he can't hear cars pull up to the house, so now I have to go to the door to greet people.

The amazing thing is, he's never slept better in his life. Before, the slightest noise sent him stalking through the house in search of a rattle in a radiator.

A creak in the pine walls of the living room or a basement pump kicking in precipitated a major fact-finding mission. Circling the house tracking the gurgling noise of rainwater through the gutters made him so dizzy he'd have to

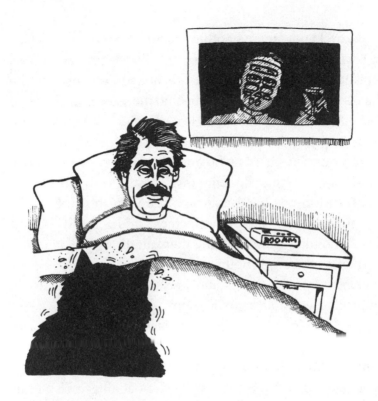

go and lie down. Now he power naps through the blasting at the nearby stone quarry.

The problem is, he *thinks* he still hears things. Like at 4 a.m. while sitting on my chest in bed, he lets out a shriek as he stares wide-eyed at the window behind my head.

Now, I know there's nothing there. I know this for a fact. But with the terror in his eyes and the death knell of his scream still echoing through the house—I'm pretty sure there's nothing in the window behind me, except . . . *Good God almighty, it's Hannibal Lecter*! He's escaped from maximum-security prison in the United States where he shared a cell with six armed guards who are now known as a casserole and he's grinning at my window in Wainfleet with a bottle of Chianti in one hand and fava beans in the other and I wheel around so fast my neck cracks and . . . and . . . and there's nothing there. Nothing there at all.

I knew there was nothing there.

And Malcolm yawns and kneads the comforter twice and collapses into a heap of sleep.

Me? I listen to talk radio until it's light outside and therefore time to get up and feed him. This is a definite disadvantage. Mine. Since he went deaf the bottom line is he's never slept better and I've hardly slept at all. And isn't this the kind of trade-off we enjoy making with our pets? And isn't there an institution somewhere we can check into for help?

Now you know why I hide behind doors and curtains during the day and scare him as often as I can—*Revenge*!

It's true that you compensate in other areas when one of your senses shuts down. An open can of sardines, for instance, can still bring Malcolm back from a foreign country. A whack on the rear end spells NO in capital letters.

And of course we sign. An extended arm and index finger means "go out." Two hands repeatedly slapped to the top of the lap means "jump up." A circular, beckoning motion with the arm means "come here." And Malcolm is probably one of the few cats in the world who has learned to sign back. Really. Simply by turning his front paw upward and extending his middle claw, he tells me just what I can do with all these orders. I think he picked up that sign while watching *Question Period* televised live from the House of Commons.

Let's see. Now he's deaf, nearly toothless, doesn't move so well and his tongue sticks stupidly out the side of his mouth. His parts seem to be falling off faster than an Edsel's in an earthquake. If Malcolm were an automobile, he'd have been made in Detroit on a Friday afternoon.

The problem is, if Malcolm were such a car, I'd probably still be his owner. My luck with cats and cars runs pretty much the same.

12
MALCOLM'S GONNA LIVE

There comes a time in every man's existence when, as much as he'd rather not, he must face the grim inevitability of death.

Not me, of course. I've already made arrangements to marry Shirley MacLaine and become a matador in Madrid about an hour after my funeral service, which I sincerely hope goes off without a hitch. There's the case—and I'm not making this up—of the butcher in England who died leaving a will with two last wishes: he wanted to be cremated and he wanted a professional piano player hired to play Cole Porter's great hit "Everytime We Say Goodbye." He got most of his request, sort of. He was cremated and a professional musician was hired to play at the ceremony. Unfortunately, the pianist had brought the wrong sheet music and at the climax of the cremation ceremony played The Platters' greatest hit, "Smoke Gets in Your Eyes." Oh, don't you just hate when that happens.

The inevitability of life's end occurred to me the other day when—while standing in front of a framed anatomical poster of the canine ear amid piles of tapeworms, bladder stones and feather ticks—Dr. David Thorne had Malcolm pinned to the stainless steel examination table, his jaws pried open wide.

Normally, Malcolm is a friendly and affectionate feline prone to loud purring and, when excited, long yangers of drool. But bring in a human in a lab coat, a paid professional at that, who's there to interrupt his eternal eat-and-sleep routine, and Malcolm is perfectly willing to hurl himself at this person and rip a vein from his neck.

First, David looked into Malcolm's mouth, the dumping ground for all things edible.

"Geez," he said, jumping back. "He's only got half a tongue!" I looked in. "Good Lord," I said, equally unbelieving. "You're right!"

Dumbfounded, we relaxed our grip and stopped for a moment of reflection while Malcolm looked from one of us to the other.

"You did that," I said in an unaccusatory tone. "A couple of years ago, when the possum bit him in the mouth and gangrene set in. You cut out half his tongue."

"Oh yeah, that's right, I did," said the doctor, remembering the ordeal.

Malcolm had that questioning, annoyed look that cats often have when they're trying to say: "Hey, what's the point of keeping files if nobody's going to refer to them before these examinations!"

We returned to our task of rending Malcolm in half by the jaws while keeping all his offensive weapons at arm's length. David is wary of his sharp teeth, particularly the one on the bottom. I keep my distance because Malcolm with his busy schedule doesn't always take time to brush after every meal. Let's just say if Dr. Ballard ever comes up with a new flavour like Listerine 'n' Liver, Malcolm is their main target market. Whereas Malcolm once stalked his prey and threatened to gum them to death, now he vaporizes them in a cloud of halitosis.

Anyway, we saw the problem, raw infested patches of flesh in the back of the mouth behind half a tongue that no longer squawked, past ridges of gums that no longer held teeth. In short order an anaesthetic was administered, a scraping done, the specimen sent to Guelph University for a biopsy with results to follow "in a few weeks."

Faced with hard, cold reality, I have resigned myself to the sad fact that after a rather tawdry life of carousing, staying out late and chasing immoral females (him, not me), Malcolm is probably going to expire someday.

This lovable little furball is now eighteen years old and I've just now noticed a thin milky film starting to gloss over his eyes.

In human years, using the ratio of 7:1, this makes Malcolm as old as France's Jean Calmet, the world's oldest surviving human being who once knew Vincent Van Gogh. And every year on her birthday they ask her: "What was Van Gogh like?"

And she replies: "He was an ugly little man with alcohol on his breath." Next question?

I always wondered how they came up with that 7:1 ratio of pet years to human years. Maybe it was a case of a seventy-year-old man and his ten-year-old tomcat both dying of old age on the very same day. (The wife and the cat's girlfriend, of course, lived to ages of ninety-one and thirteen respectively.)

Cats are such wonderful watchers of everything around them that maybe they get a real good look at people and their lives and the 7:1 ratio is self-imposed. They just refuse to go to 8:1.

Probably it was the result of two third-year veterinary students partway through a case of beer with a thesis deadline hanging over their heads:

"What are we going to write about?"

"Have you noticed how cats don't live as long as people?"

"Perfect. The James Dean Syndrome applied to cats, man. All the good ones go early."

"Nah, it's got to be more scientific, with theories and numbers and stuff."

"That's a great idea, man. How many beers have you had, anyway?"

"Seven."

"That's it—seven to one, cats to people. Sign it here at the bottom and I'll drop it off in the morning."

I'll never know how they came up with this arbitrary rate of aging, but I did know how to prepare myself for the unavoidable. So I called a local insurance company to get one of those huge policies on Malcolm's life, the kind Roy Rogers got for Trigger, the kind Imelda got for Ferdinand.

The woman on the phone seemed a little confused. "Is Malcolm like your son, or what?"

Thank God for bad grammar, I didn't have to lie. After eighteen years, $8,840 in food bills and $4,348.56 in medical expenses, Malcolm was more like my son than a real son, if I had a son and he was kind of pudgy and accident-prone.

In order to give me a cost estimate, she started down the questions on the insurance application. We breezed through "date of birth" and "nationality," then "marital status" and "present occupation" came up. "Single/spayed and recently retired," I replied.

Then it got tough. At "height in shoes" and "weight in ordinary clothes" I had to tell her I'd call her right back.

Off the phone, I paced and Malcolm circled. What to wear? What to wear? I tried to remember what Trigger was wearing in the last photo I saw of him, but somehow I could not imagine Malcolm draped in a hand-tooled leather saddle and Dale Evans.

I chose a pair of black and white saddle shoes, a polo shirt with the collar up and a cardigan sweater. I started to put a pair of cords on him and then I thought: How ridiculous! We're doing this by phone, for gawdsakes!

(Just for the record, I own a cat who stands 32 centimetres in saddle shoes, weighs 26 kilograms in an Irish-knit cardigan that makes him look like Perry Como had Perry been born into a litter of six scruffy urchins by a morally bankrupt mother and a father who split even before the panting subsided.)

"He's not very big, is he?" she asked.

"No, not in metric," I replied.

We moved down the list, checking "No" beside all the things near and dear to an insurance salesman's heart: persistent hoarseness, asthma, blood-spitting, bronchitis, jaundice, gall-bladder problems, chronic diarrhea, urinary swelling, convulsions . . . Boy, a little shop talk over dinner with these guys must be an experience and a half. I'd just love to see an office interview with a recently arrived immigrant in which the insurance salesman had to act all these things out.

Just the other side of dizziness, fainting and recurrent headaches, we hit an impasse known as "history of mental illness." I looked at Malcolm. Malcolm grinned.

"What's the penalty for perjury?" I asked.

"Are you lying?" asked the secretary.

"No, I am not lying. Did I say I was lying? Are you accusing me of lying?"

I heard her make three checkmarks in the family history column beside "nervous anxiety," chronic paranoia" and "borderline schizophrenia."

I don't mind fudging the facts a little, but if you think I'm going to certify the mental soundness of a cat who once spent the Victoria Day weekend staring down a drainpipe in my neighbour's flowerbed, then you must think I'm crazy.

This is the same cat who one day, while looking for a new place to nap, dove into the toilet not knowing I'd left the seat up, and I'm going to sign a document that says mentally he's just fine? Who's certifying who here?

"During the last five years has your son used hallucino-genic or habit-forming drugs?" she asked.

"Does catnip count?"

"I'll be hanging up now," she said. And she did.

Waiting for those test results was hell around the house, a silence rife with regrets and unrequited wishes.

I'd be leafing through an atlas when Malcolm would suddenly jump into my lap and put his paw on a far-off land he'd probably never get to visit.

He rolled over on his back a lot, making obvious by its absence the manhood I had had removed so many years ago. He hauled out all his old cat toys and left them in the middle of the room, a rusting heap of mechanical mice and battery-driven birds, no kitten to pass them on to.

He ate slowly for a change, thoughtfully savouring every morsel as though this meal might be his last.

He went for a field trip in the neighbourhood, hoping to make peace with old enemies, but alas, he had outlived almost all of them.

One night I caught him down on the beach staring aimlessly across still waters at a lighthouse beacon on distant shores near Dunkirk, New York. That's when I called Dr. Thorne. When a cat comes to that point in his life when he contemplates Dunkirk, New York, it's probably all over but the meowing.

Dr. Thorne had good news and bad. Good news: "Malcolm's going to live," he said, with excitement and warmth in his voice. And the bad news? "Malcolm's going to live," he said, with a certain amount of resignation. (Did I mention how perceptive a veterinarian Dr. Thorne is?)

All right! Those five weeks of fighting to get a pill down his throat first thing in the morning had paid off. (Getting the pill into his mouth was tough, but getting him to drink the glass of water was murder.)

But yes! Malcolm will live to litter another box, to throw yet another hairball, to torture one more toad.

Malcolm lives! Dead and decaying rodents, beware!

Send me those mounting medical bills, Dr. David Thorne! Put on a midnight shift, you people at Miss Mew! Hear me, Hartz—more flea shampoo, two-in-one collars, litter, leashes, two ounces of Colombian catnip and one of those plastic spiders that skitters across the kitchen floor on penlight batteries!

The news was too good to keep to myself. "Hi Mom— could you loan me $864.76 for the next year? Malcolm's gonna live!"

He's such a treasure to me. I don't know what I'd do without him except maybe eat out in a restaurant once in a while or buy myself a new baseball glove.

13
MALCOLM, MARG
AND ME

Sometimes, subconsciously, we choose to ignore the painfully obvious.

You just know the economy is bad when the government tells you to tighten your belt and you can't because you're using it to hold down the tarp on the roof. I mean you know things are rough when you go into Eaton's to buy a shirt and the saleman's not actually wearing one.

But I never fully appreciated how tough times really were until my mother showed up on my doorstep with all her worldly belongings.

Yes, my mother has come to live with me, temporarily. (Temporarily—adverb, from the word *temporal*, meaning of limited time, for a brief period, transiently, June 15 tops!)

When she called and said she was moving because she needed a cheaper place to live, I said, "Great!" I thought she meant Florida. Mentally I had my tennis rackets restrung and I was time-sharing the spare room of her condo well into next winter.

When she asked if it would be all right if she moved in here with me, I took one of those laughing fits where the tears stream down your face and you can't quite catch your breath. (Malcolm thought I was going into cardiac arrest, so he dialled 811. I know, I know . . . never trust a cat to save your life in an emergency.)

End thirteen years of living alone in a house where music is a must but clothes are merely optional? Give up a life of weird hours, strange friends, good wine and bad diet? What a sense of humour this woman has.

It's odd that upon seeing her at the door last week with all her worldly belongings, the laughter subsided but the tears were back in full force.

We discussed several options before I actually opened the door: my oldest sister's condo in Toronto, a senior's apartment, the bus station, a job as a roadie with the Rolling Stones. Then my mother produced a document that a lawyer declared legal and binding when I described it to him on the phone—a document that listed me as the mortgagee and her as the mortgagor.

Damn. It was good to see her again. Not since the renewal at $9\,1/2$ per cent had I realized how I'd missed this woman. (Mortgage—noun, from the word *mort*, meaning till death do you pay and then only on the interest.)

So now there are three of us. Malcolm is 126 in human years and Marg is eighty-five, also in human years. Not to dwell on my mother's age but to put it in historical context, the year my mother was born Sir Wilfrid Laurier was a prime minister, not a university, the Kenora Thistles won the Stanley

Cup and Jack Miner was standing by a pond near Kingsville, Ontario, throwing bread at goose decoys and mumbling, "If you feed them, they will come."

Now don't get me wrong, she looks like she's in her low seventies, but the fact remains she dated William the Conqueror.

It's been several months now, and don't misunderstand me, we *are* all getting along. Like three fish in a shot glass.

Essentially I have two roommates whose combined age is a robust 211 years. And this poses no problem whatsoever unless of course you want to do something a little on the adventurous side—like communicate. Example:

Me: "Get off the couch."

Mom: "What?"

Me: "I told him to get off the couch."

Mom: "Why, I'm not hurting anything!"

Me: "Not you—him."

Malcolm contributes one wheeze and two sighs to this conversation and shifts so that all four paws are now straight up in the air.

The phrases "Huh?" and "Whadyasay?" seem to dominate all household conversations these days, and Malcolm has his head cocked in that inquisitive pose so often we're not sure if his vertebrae have fused or he's impersonating the RCA Victor dog.

We have moments, the three of us, of which memories are made.

Me: "I gotta go to the store and get some litter so I can clean out Malcolm's box. Do we need milk?"

Mom: "I just cleaned out the fridge yesterday, dear."

Me: "I said the litter box, not the fridge!"

Mom: "Well that's a stupid place to keep milk!"

When they film my mother's life story it'll star one of the Cordick sisters in a two-part Lenny's—I mean Denny's—commercial.

Meanwhile, Malcolm paces back and forth between the litter box and the fridge not knowing what he should do if an opportunity arises at either location. His mind races back and forth between a bowl of milk and a bowel movement until he works himself into a nap.

And hearing problems? It's an eerie feeling to be sitting in a party of three and you're the only one who hears the phone ringing. And when you get up to answer it, both of them look at you like you're psychic.

Sometimes I'll answer the phone when it hasn't been ringing and I'll proceed to have a loud, animated conversation with an editor or a producer and I'll use coarse language and tell him as a writer I'm just not going to take it anymore. When I return, they both seem pleased I stuck up for myself, and Lord knows I feel a lot better.

My mother never cared for cats, but she absolutely loves Malcolm. She'll talk to him and play with him and then she'll rough him up a little too much and Malcolm will rake her hand with his claws. That's usually when I walk in.

They both look guilty—one's bleeding, the other's cowering. I want to send them both to bed without their dinners. Or better yet, switch their dinners.

I don't know who to trust anymore. I'm sure she's sneaking him treats when I'm not home and I'd bet money it was Malcolm who tipped my mother off to the beer fridge in the basement. Just because I'm not naturally a paranoid person, it doesn't mean at least one of them isn't out to get me.

More than once I've thought of taking out one of those "Free to a Good Home" notices, and frankly I'd just as soon flip a coin to choose which name appears in the ad, Marg or Malcolm Thomas.

Call me crazy, but I don't think a man forty-five years of age should have to hide the *Playboy* magazine under the sofa every time his mother walks in the room. Yesterday I found the swimsuit issue of *Fab Felines* under Malcolm's litter box, so he must be feeling the pressure as well.

On the bright side, both Malcolm and I are looking forward to growing up tall and strong now that we're eating all our greens, and we're equally astonished at how much dirt had accumulated behind our ears during the time we were baching it.

The situation, however, is not without humour. The first day I watched Malcolm brushing after every meal, I damn near hurt myself laughing.

It was around that time that I read about an interesting phenomenon evolving in Japan, as if anything that develops in a country where they feed beer to beef cattle and raw fish to people is not at the very least interesting.

It seems the Japanese are burned out and succumbing to stress-related diseases because they work fourteen-hour days producing expensive electronic gadgets that we Canadians buy in one minute with a credit card and then work overtime and part-time paying off our debts. (Boy, those Japanese aren't exactly as clever as we think, eh?)

The article revealed that the Japanese population is rapidly aging, and with their children off chasing the almighty yen, the older folks are lonely. That's why a personal service company in Tokyo is offering to rent—I'm not making this up—a "stand-in" family to lonesome Japanese couples to fill the void left by their real family. The fee for these "entertainers" is $1,300 for a half day of companionship and communication.

I tried to imagine what kind of people would *rent* family members out to strangers for monetary gain. Had the devaluation of human life finally come to this? Did that company in Tokyo think for one minute they could just run an ad in a newspaper and find "spare" family members who would just pick up and . . . did they even once consider the feelings of . . . did anybody not notice the . . .

I had the woman in the classified section of the local newspaper on the phone within minutes and reading my ad back to me:

> Are you a little lonesome these days? Just the two of you in that big old house with nobody to talk to? Could you use a little company and light entertainment? Do you have cash? For less than $300 a day you could rent MARGARET AND MALCOLM—a congenial couple of cut-ups known professionally as THE LADY AND THE TRAMP. She does magic tricks! He sleeps through

them! They both love ice cream! Call now. Operators are standing by.

The ad wasn't what you'd call successful, but the offer still stands. And if you're interested in renting my family and you phone and get my answering machine, I've worked out a system to handle my calls and those calls that are for my mom. If the message is for me just say it's for William Thomas and if it's for Marg you could also just say it's for William Thomas because *she listens in on the extension!*

It's a shame the print ad didn't work because I was going to follow it up with a promotional video on the MuchMusic cable station featuring Annie Lennox of The Eurythmics. I envisioned a fast-paced, action-packed little music movie starring Margaret and Malcolm and entitled *The Arthritics*. "Coming soon to a sofa near you!"

Of course I'm just kidding. There are a lot of advantages having my mom living with me.

For instance, it's a real time saver to sit down at the end of each day with the crossword puzzle and find out it's already done.

Our electricity bill has dropped significantly since my mother moved in. There's no need to leave a light on while

I'm out, now that there's somebody standing at the door, looking at her watch and tapping her foot every night when I come home.

I've lost weight. Who can find time for food when it's tea time twenty-four hours a day?

And, of course, I spend more quality time with Malcolm now that he's chosen to hide out in the same place as I do: the tool shed.

But I cannot get angry, because my mother is the sweetest and kindest woman on earth next to Mother Teresa. In fact, I've offered several times to put her on the Vatican's list for beatification, but she flatly refuses.

"They charge too much, dear," she likes to say. "I'll just get your sister to give me a perm."

Is it any wonder I love this woman? She's a saint.

And I've become more accommodating and flexible as a result of our communal living arrangement. I really have. For instance, just to ease the tension around here I've planned a family outing for next week. Friday I'll be taking Marg and Malcolm to the zoo. And if everything goes as planned, I'll pick them up the following Thursday.

Getting along just fine, we are, like three peas in a Cuisinart.

14

MALCOLM
1974–1992

Life can be so quirky, its treasures can vanish so quickly.

When tests were done to diagnose the eosinophilic ulcer in Malcolm's mouth, some imperfect indicators of aging came back with the report. Though the ulcer was cleared right up with hormone injections, his urea nitrogen count remained high, almost as high as his creatinine level. The aging process had cost Malcolm a significant loss of kidney and liver functions, resulting in a buildup of toxins in his bloodstream. But it was far from critical, and cats, I was told, could function normally for years with as little as 10 or 15 per cent of their kidney and liver functions.

We put him on a strict low-protein diet with a schedule of regular checkups to monitor his system. It was a good plan, except that he never made it to his next regular checkup. Long before he was due I took him in on an emergency basis when he suddenly quit eating. When Malcolm refuses food, alarm bells go off in my head as well as in the offices of several major suppliers of canned food and cat treats.

Dr. Thorne's first question to me was about drinking too much and frequent urination. I admitted he was right, but told him I had hoped that we could focus immediately on Malcolm's problems and discuss my lifestyle later.

The next day or two are just a blur now: dismal, dreadful days of hoping beyond hope and trying to spot a high point on the horizon, just beyond reality.

Malcolm wouldn't eat his low-protein food, but he still couldn't resist a little bit of tuna, a very high-protein product. I always knew that raw life always came down to tough choices, but I never thought it would come in a six-ounce can marked "flaked" or "chunk." Feed him tuna and overwork what little was left of his kidney and liver function, or withhold food and watch him waste away?

In the end it didn't seem to matter. Dr. Thorne said he'd never seen a cat deteriorate so rapidly after tests had shown the problem was far from life-threatening. His organs just shut down.

All but one. His little heart wouldn't quit as I and the good doctor sincerely hoped it would.

The last time I had him in, David asked to keep him at the clinic and put him to sleep, but I took him home instead. Malcolm was not in agony or any obvious pain, he was just fading so very fast . . . I wanted him for one more night.

Malcolm slept that night where he almost always slept, in the well of my chest and arms with his head on the edge of the pillow. It was almost a perfect last-night's sleep, interrupted only be Malcolm's insistence at 5 a.m. on walking down the hall to the litter box to take a pee.

In the event of an emergency, I had set out a litter box in the bedroom with paper all around it, but no, he insisted on going where he'd always gone, where he'd been trained to go. That walk down the hall—Malcolm wobbling and nearly falling, me on hands and knees crawling beside him to keep him from falling down—that walk down the hall was as close to hell as I hope I ever get. It took forever, and when it was over I was a lot more drained than he was.

But he did it, all the way down and all the way back, and when I put him back in bed it was a question of which one of us was proudest. Malcolm showed me more courage and class in that trip for his predawn tinkle than Lassie did in seventeen years of prime-time television.

To the end he was determined to be a good and loyal pet and no problem to me whatsoever. To the end, he was that and much, much more.

At 8 a.m. we had a little talk and said our good-byes. It went better than I expected until one of us broke down and cried.

Dave Thorne and his assistant came out shortly after that. I wasn't sure which of us was more upset, me or Malcolm's vet.

"It's like losing a member of your family," he said to me, so sensitive after having to do this so many times.

"David," I said, "obviously you don't know my family." Let's give Uncle Ranald the needle, I thought, and save that little bugger in the bedroom.

But it couldn't be done, and I wandered off to sit on my breakwall and stare off over the lake at nothing whatsoever. David found Malcolm in bed half asleep and with the deft and tender hands of a healer, he made that sleep deeper and sweeter and more restful than Malcolm had ever experienced. It was the big sleep Malcolm had earned all his life and now so richly deserved. People should be so lucky.

I couldn't hang around the house that day and it was just as well. I had a very important meeting in Toronto. It was a meeting with my publisher, to sign the contract for a book. A book entitled *Malcolm and Me: Life in the Litter Box*.

Yes, life is nothing if it's not perversely eventful.

Today is actually the first day I've spent at home alone in eighteen years. And you know, it's the funniest thing. The electric can opener whines and spins and no little creature attacks my ankles. I open the fridge to get a beer and a small ball of fur doesn't stick his face in to inspect the state of supplies. I walk by a dining-room chair and no paw shoots out to catch my pant leg, no head bumps the bottom of the table. The only thing at the foot of the bed is a comforter, and it doesn't fight me for space or creep up and curl up on my chest. Nothing follows me out to the breakwall, the same little nothing doesn't race me back to the kitchen door—loser pours the milk.

I'll have to buy an alarm clock now. As I may have mentioned, I'm not a morning person, but my cat sure was.

It occurs to me from everywhere and everything I see and touch that Malcolm is gone.

Not a day went by that he didn't make me curse or smile or laugh and often all three at once.

Malcolm wasn't a handsome cat, not unless you're a person who could see beauty in a face with an overbite and the tip of the tongue semi-permanently sticking out the side of his mouth. But I thought he was handsome.

Malcolm wasn't a classically marked cat. His black-on-grey stripes looked like they were painted on by a guy with a good sense of humour but a bad case of DTs. But I read a lot between those lines.

Physically, Malcolm looked like an ad for no-fault insurance. He wobbled from side to side when he walked, the John Wayne swagger with Slinky-toy momentum.

Emotionally, he was stable with a bit of a temper and intellectually he was smarter than anybody now running or planning to run this country. Malcolm ran this house, and when he left there was both unity and assets that will produce dividends for years to come. The advance on his book alone is enough to re-establish my credit line at the Belmont Hotel. I don't mean to brag, but fiscal responsibility in a cat is a rare thing indeed.

(Author's note: When I say "Malcolm ran this house" I don't mean *he ran this house*. It's just the kind of thing cat lovers like to hear. No, in fact I pride myself in knowing that our entire relationship was a grand plan made possible when a superior intellect managed to first identify and later control the responses of an animal further down the scale of social development utilizing a very basic system of rewarding treats interspersed by periodic scoldings. Don't misunderstand this, it wasn't total domination. Sometimes he let me sleep in on Sundays, and he never once made mention of all the wine bottles in the Blue Box.)

So he wasn't pretty or poised or the pride of his species, but that little rake could eat his way out of a cave-in at the cat food factory and go back in to rescue a six-pack for the road. Malcolm had an appetite that you could tease twice a day but never actually satisfy.

Looking back over his rap sheet, I realize how most of Malcolm's crimes were food-related. The frequent breaking into the kitchen trash bin for chicken bones, the shredding of plastic garbage bags in the shed for clam shells, the shattering of the bird feeder for stale bread—all of these transgressions were the acts of an addict crying out for help . . . and anything remotely edible.

With a penchant for trouble and a nose for nutrition, Malcolm was the only cat I know who spent most of his life in the dog house.

Okay, so if he wasn't well groomed, well behaved or well anything, what exactly was he?

Malcolm was a piece of work.

He could purr a person out of a depression, drool on your chest until you dreamed you were drowning, talk you out of your TV snack and invariably worm himself into a position directly between you and whatever you were reading. Malcolm turned annoying and nauseating into respected art forms.

Malcolm started out as a scrawny little runt too shy and too skittery to come out of a garage apartment I lived in near a highway in Fonthill. Here at the lake he blossomed into the King of Sunset Bay, patrolling a seven-cottage territory with authority, an uninvited regular at neighbourhood barbecues.

At dawn Malcolm would stalk Sunset Bay, terrorizing two square miles of semi-wilderness like a raging Bengal tiger. By ten-thirty he'd have to come in the house to take a leak. It was never easy being King of the Jungle with weak kidneys.

The past few summers he was my shadow on midnight walks along the beach. If I'd have had him for one more summer there's no doubt I could have taught him how to carry a brandy snifter and hold a cigar during those walks.

As a cat he dug more than his share of holes in his life. (I know, I stepped in a few barefoot.) But no hole was bigger than the one he left in mine.

They take up so little room in your house, pets do. They leave such a huge and hollow gap when they're gone.

Malcolm's up there now, in human heaven. (Other pets couldn't put up with him for more than a few minutes. There's no chance he'd be let into their heaven.) So if you go before I do—or, as is more than likely the case, if I'm offered the escalator to the basement instead of the elevator to the penthouse—remember, he gets half a tin in the morning, half a tin at supper and cat treats only if he's behaving himself. A little milk for an extraordinary accomplishment wouldn't hurt either.

And don't fall for those big green eyes or that rubbing up against your leg routine, or the tap on the nose when you're napping. Give in once to Malcolm, just once, and in a week he'll be wearing your halo.

EPILOGUE

Under the gun, most of us are just no good whatsoever.

Years ago I interviewed a crusty, aging Welland lawyer who gave me a lot of advice, most of which I never asked for. I let him ramble on only after he promised he wouldn't bill me. The lawyer was a tough old buzzard who had a reputation as a good sailor and an impossible boss. He was still going into the office every day at age ninety-one.

"Never trust the human mind in a crisis," he said to me. "It's liable to do the damnedest things."

He went on to recall how he was sailing off Point Abino, on Lake Erie, one day with his second wife when a sudden squall came up and an unusually powerful wave hit the boat broadside.

"Knocked the wife clear out of the boat," he said, his eyebrows rising with the impact of this incident so very long ago. "And do you know what I did," he asked, "me at the helm and her in the drink?"

"No," I replied, "what did you do?"

"I turned the boat around and picked her up . . . Never trust the human mind in a crisis, son, it's liable to do the damnedest things!"

I thought about that pearl of wisdom while stumbling around in a haze of hurt after Malcolm's death.

I was stunned by the reactions of readers after Malcolm's obituary ran in my weekly syndicated column "All the World's a Circus."

I received sympathy cards, bereavement poems, photographs of people's cats, long and personal letters and much much more.

A woman—Ninalee Allen Craig—in Burlington, Ontario, purchased a tree, in Malcolm's name, in a new conservation area there. I thought that was kind of ironic: Malcolm couldn't climb a tree when he was alive, and now dead, he owns one.

Pamela Wylie of Hamilton made a sizeable donation in Malcolm's name to the Pet Trust Fund at the Ontario Veterinary Medical Association in Guelph, Ontario. I can't tell you the hours I've spent trying to have this money re-routed from Malcolm's account through the Cayman Islands and into my personal chequing account here in Wainfleet. Apparently they have certain rules and regulations.

The outpouring of compassion was truly comforting but I discouraged any mourning either by readers or myself. Pity is ill-placed on a cat like Malcolm who had a full and happy life of shelter, love and food. Most people should be so lucky.

Two messages from readers really hit home. The first was from someone called Brian.

"Thanks for your column on Malcolm. I cried so much while reading it. With so much hatred in the world it's nice to know that someone else can understand the meaning of love. P.S. My wife cried, too."

I want you to know that Brian and I have now recovered from our moments of weakness and we're big, tough guys again enjoying violence in hockey and denying that tears have ever touched our cheeks.

A Jackie Pfander sent a letter of condolence, and added: "P.S. When my husband came in, I said, 'Malcolm died.' He replied, 'Oh, no. What a shame,' instead of saying 'Malcolm who?' That in itself is quite a tribute, wouldn't you say?"

Yes, Jackie, I'd say so.

I wasn't myself in those early hours of mourning and some of my actions proved it.

I should apologize to Dr. David Thorne. Only half listening to him when he was detailing Malcolm's diagnosis the day before he died, I heard him say the word *transplant*. I rushed over to him, embraced him and thanked him a thousand times. I misunderstood. David wasn't offering one of his organs, he was merely pointing out the gravity of the situation by saying that if Malcolm were a human, only a transplant would save him.

I'm so embarrassed. Even after I understood, I asked David for his liver. Sorry, David.

I should apologize to my friend, Don Bastian, who edited the original version of *Malcolm and Me*. I mentioned that the contract signing with my publisher took place only hours after we put Malcolm to sleep. But I didn't, I couldn't, tell anybody at the publishing house that Malcolm had died that morning. My immediate goal was to get through the day without falling apart in public, and of course there was also the matter of money. I wasn't so sure my cheque would be torn up and I'd be tossed out of the boardroom had they known the subject had expired that morning. Now I know that would never have happened. Sorry, Don.

The people at the publishing house are kind and friendly, and more than one came forth to ask: "So how's Malcolm?"

"Well, he's sure slowed down a lot lately," I said without actually telling a lie. Sorry, Don.

Finally I must apologize to Malcolm. Long ago I had decided that I would keep Malcolm's ashes. This is one of those ideas that sounds good only at the time. Carrying it off is quite another story. First there's a pickup at the clinic, then a drop-off to a Humane Society in another town, then a decision to be made on communal cremation versus a single ceremony with rates that escalate accordingly, and finally a delivery of the ashes.

Mistakes could be made, I thought, identities could be mixed up. Finally I decided to handle it myself. I'd have a top-drawer single cremation and I'd do the delivery and pickup with no possibility of a foul-up. I have a very good friend in the funeral business, and after hearing some of the handling mistakes made with human bodies, well, I'd just see this one through myself.

The problem was, from the morning he died to the Sunday set for private cremations, I had a four-day wait. I was determined to make things as private as possible, so I refused the offer of refrigeration facilities at the veterinary clinic. I was already at an impasse. And then it dawned on me—hell, I own two fridges!

And so it was before I set out for Toronto and the meeting with my publisher that I bundled Malcolm up in his favourite blanket, then into a plastic bag I secured with bungee cords, and then I gently and respectfully deposited him in the fridge.

Suddenly I was overcome with a tearful fit of laughter. Malcolm in death had been granted the one wish he'd been denied in life—to spend four full days in the fridge. Never trust the human mind in a crisis, son . . .

Okay, so it happened to be my beer fridge in the basement, but it was kind of fitting all the same. (Those four days, by the way, eclipsed the previous record of three consecutive days spent in my beer fridge established by my former neighbour Murray the Cop. The only difference being that Murray came out for air once in a while.)

My biggest fear was that my mother, Margaret, who was staying with me at the time would slip downstairs for a cold beer, open the fridge, and . . . and I'd lose two loved ones in one day.

All things considered, it was the best I could do under the circumstances, Malcolm. Sorry.

Somehow, not smoothly or smartly or anything remotely related to grace under fire, we muddle through life's crises. And it all worked out. I am now the proud possessor of a special mahogany urn made by a sympathetic wood sculptor in

Forrestville, New York. And soon Malcolm will take his rightful place, front and centre on the mantel over my fireplace, upon the dedication of this book.

For some strange reason my mind, calmer and out of crisis, wandered back along happy trails to Roy Rogers. Humming "Happy Trails to You," I remembered how Roy had his horse, Trigger, stuffed and put on display in the foyer of his home. I still have trouble believing anybody would stuff a pet, but that's exactly what Roy did. If you went to Roy Rogers' house today you'd be greeted by this muscle-bound stallion, rearing up on his back legs, ready to kick the gun out of your hand.

I remember once hearing Dale Evans on a radio talk show. The host asked her *why*.

"Why in the world would Roy stuff Trigger?" He asked.

"Because," replied Dale very enthusiastically, "Roy just loved him so much."

Every time I passed Malcolm's ashes on the mantel I would have a good thought for Dale Evans. I can't tell you how relieved I was that in the end, Roy passed away before Dale did. I know how much he loved her.

P.S.

When *Malcolm and Me—Life in the Litter Box* hit the bookstores in Canada in the fall, the people in charge of categorizing books placed it in the section entitled NATURE. And there it stayed for most of its shelf life.

I was a little upset until I learned that the same people had placed W.O. Mitchell's book *The Black Bonspeil of Willy McCrimmon* under Black Studies. Douglas Gibson's book on genealogy *In Search of Your Roots* ended up under the hanging store sign . . . you guessed . . . GARDENING.

So Malcolm and me were hidden away in NATURE. This was, as I mentioned, the same cat who was out the door at the crack of dawn to stalk the neighbourhood like a Bengal Tiger on a high-protein diet but had to be back in the house by 10:30 a.m. to take a leak. Suffice to say, Malcolm had more in common with the Discovery Channel than he did nature.